SELECTED POEMS

Th

GW00504165

ALSO BY DANIEL WEISSBORT
from Carcanet

Nietzsche's Attaché Case

Nikolay Zabolotsky

Selected Poems

TRANSLATED FROM THE RUSSIAN

Edited by Daniel Weissbort

CARCANET

Published in Great Britain in 1999 by
Carcanet Press Limited
4th Floor Conavon Court
12–16 Blackfriars Street
Manchester M3 5BQ

A CIP catalogue record for this book
is available from the British Library.
ISBN 1 85754 403 X

The publisher acknowledges financial
assistance from the Arts Council of England.

Set in Ehrhardt by XL Publishing Services, Tiverton
Printed and bound in Great Britain by SRP Ltd, Exeter

dedicated to the memory of
Ted Hughes
and
Joseph Brodsky

Contents

Nikolay Alekseyevich Zabolotsky
(1903–1958)

Robin Milner-Gulland

The life and work of Nikolay Zabolotsky provide a remarkable example of the power of the literary – specifically, poetic – vocation. How this came to be so is far from obvious. He did not emerge from the Moscow or Petersburg literary intelligentsia, but was born into a family that had only just risen above its peasant origins, and grew up in a village (Sernur) and small town (Urzhum) in what was even for Russia the exceptionally out-of-the-way and rural Vyatka province. His father was a local agronomist (agricultural adviser) with a taste for homespun philosophizing, his mother had been a schoolteacher, there were books in the house, and by the age of seven, apparently, Zabolotsky had chosen his future career. He got a good but not remarkable education in the Urzhum secondary school, and became an indigent student first of medicine in Moscow, then of literature at the Herzen Educational Institute in Petrograd, during the famine-stricken years immediately after the Revolution. Though briefly tempted by academic life, he was determined to be (and with some hardships became) a professional writer. Thereafter he pursued his mission with an innate stubbornness that eventually jeopardized his life and probably saved it too: he was arrested in 1938, spent six and a half years in prison and two more in exile, but survived and (perhaps uniquely) managed to re-establish himself afterwards as a writer. Personally unobtrusive, courteous and fastidious, of clerkly demeanour, the very opposite of the popular notion of the inspired Bohemian, he was driven till, literally, his last day of life by the overwhelming sense of what he could do, and what it was his responsibility to do, in poetry.

Since Zabolotsky's manner of writing changed more than once, apparently abruptly and mysteriously, to the extent that one (well-disposed) critic could assert that 'unlike Akhmatova or Mandelshtam, Zabolotsky is moved by nothing other than the desire to write', his consistent single-mindedness of purpose deserves further scrutiny. His aims seem to have been at all periods fundamentally cognitive: poetry was to him a special kind of, or route to, knowledge. In his last full year of life he wrote notes (probably for lectures) that state the writer's purpose in terms that would not have been inappropriate for the Formalists of the 1920s: 'the genuine artist strips objects and phenomena of their everyday coverings and speaks to the reader: "those things that you have become used to seeing daily, over whose surfaces your habituated and indifferent gaze slides, are really far from ordinary, far from everyday, but full of inexplicable delight"...' To achieve his purposes, 'the poet works with all his being simultaneously: with reason, heart, soul and muscles. He works with all his organism, and the more harmoniously integrated this work, the higher its quality. For thought to triumph he embodies it in images. For language to work he draws from it all its musical might. Thought – Image – Music: that is the ideal trinity towards which the poet strives.'

The cognitive purpose and method remained constant: the objects of cognition and the stylistic means employed for its realization underwent remarkable transformations. (Perhaps this is appropriate, since transformation or 'metamorphoses' – the title of a fine poem of 1937 [included here] – are among Zabolotsky's constant themes.) A frequent catalyst for changes of style or subject-matter would be encounters with writers, thinkers or their works: 'as far as people and books are concerned, I have struck very lucky', he wrote. The most crucial early encounter came in the mid-1920s when he met Daniil Kharms and Aleksandr Vvedensky, with whom in 1928 he founded the OBERIU group of writers and performers. He rejected his early work, imitating as he said now Blok, now Akhmatova, now Mayakovsky, now Yesenin, and sank himself in the composition of a cycle of highly idiosyncratic, fragmented, grotesque pictures of Leningrad life under NEP, that were to become the central element of his slim first book, *Stolbtsy* (*Columns* or *Scrolls*, 1929), which propelled him into instant notoriety. At that stage press criticism could be shrugged off; less than a decade later it might lead to arrest, even (perhaps particularly) in the case of a fundamentally apolitical writer such as Zabolotsky. In the 1920s his fantastical imagination brought him (and his friends) an invitation from the poet Samuil Marshak to work in children's literature, which provided his means of livelihood till translations, above all from Georgian, took over. As for OBERIU – whose manifesto Zabolotsky largely wrote – it was effectively snuffed out in 1930, though its members and supporters continued to meet informally (e.g. in Leonid Lipavsky's 'Club of Semi-Literate Scholars', a curious discussion-group that gave rise to Zabolotsky's poem 'Time' [not included here]) for some years.

Zabolotsky's early work is often described as "belated Futurism", though he was choosy among his contemporaries (he admired in particular Khlebnikov and Mandelshtam, later Pasternak, but rejected Mayakovsky and his followers, not to mention the whole of Symbolism, peasant poetry etc.). He was at home among classically-minded figures of the past: Tyutchev, Boratynsky, Pushkin, Goethe (he knew German), and eighteenth-century writing, particularly the dialogues of Skovoroda. But visual artists were just as important to him, and the greatest personal example was set by Pavel Filonov (1883–1941), the ascetic, obsessive and charismatic painter whose theory of 'madeness' led to an utterly individual yet self-abnegating art of intense analysis. Following his father's interests he was equally concerned with the natural sciences (particularly biology and ecology): here the major influence was another ascetic eccentric, Konstantin Tsiolkovsky (father of Russian rocket technology and cosmology), with whom he corresponded. By the 1930s urban grotesquerie was displaced in his work by a concern with the natural world, the ordering of mankind's place in it, the metamorphoses between animate and inanimate being, and the meaning of death. It led to a more ordered poetic texture (though without eliminating strangeness of diction and perception); among several long poems 'Triumph of Agriculture' (here titled 'Agriculture Triumphant') caused a particular stir as it was taken as a lampoon on collectivization, and was partly responsible for his arrest.

Many Leningrad writers were arrested early in 1938 in connection with a supposed counter-revolutionary plot 'led' by N. Tikhonov (who actually remained at liberty). Zabolotsky was lucky to escape with his life, after serious maltreatment and a spell in a prison psychiatric ward. He refused to confess or make any denunciations, and was sentenced to five years in the camps (such sentences were nearly always extended in the circumstances of World War II). He and his family never stopped trying to get the sentence revoked, and this may have assisted his eventual release (it was some time before he managed to secure permission to live in Moscow). He wrote a sober yet hair-raising account of his arrest and interrogation ('History of my Imprisonment' – a classic of its kind [see pp. 203–16]), not published until long after his death. He survived imprisonment partly through getting a job as a draughtsman on the new BAM railway in the Far East, but hard labour on logging and particularly soda-extraction in the Kazakh steppe permanently undermined his health.

Imprisonment virtually stopped his poetic activity, but on release (while still in exile) he resumed translation work on his classic version of the medieval *Igor Tale*, and in the late 1940s wrote some fine original poems still in the mode of his work of the 1930s. Then he fell almost silent for the final Stalin years. He always found it hard to get his work published, and much did not appear in print in his lifetime; Soviet literary officialdom did its best to ignore the existence of his disturbing and obscure early work. In the 'Thaw' of the mid-1950s, however, he found a new and fluent voice, and a small measure of public acclaim; in 1957 he was invited on his one visit abroad, to Italy. His late poems seem lucid and formally conventional. Social and personal themes appear (there is even a cycle of unusual love-poems, 'Last Love' [included here]), but the old strangenesses of perception, and quest for cognition, are not far beneath the surface. His last major work is the cycle 'Rubruk in Mongolia' (not included here), based on the journey of the historical thirteenth-century monk Rubrucius, witty and ironical while essentially serious, reminding us that for all his sobriety of countenance and formality in behaviour this enigmatic figure was full of fun, and had indeed written some of the wittiest light and occasional verse in Russian (little of which, alas, has survived). Underrated and often mocked – in Russia and abroad – during his lifetime, Zabolotsky is generally understood to be among the great luminaries of Russian modernism, to have set a personal example few could match, and to be one of the main influences on the generation of Russian writers to have come to maturity in the last couple of decades.

SELECT BIBLIOGRAPHY

N.A. Zabolotsky, *Sobranie sochineniy* (3 vols., Moscow, 1983–4)

——, (ed. N.N. Zabolotsky), *Ogon, mertsayushchiy v sosude...* (selected works, biographical commentary, Moscow 1995)

——, 'The Story of My Imprisonment', trans. & ed. R. Milner-Gulland, *Times Literary Supplement*, 9 Oct. 1981 (reprinted here)

——, *Scrolls*, trans. & ed. D. Weissbort (Jonathan Cape, 1971)

N.N. Zabolotsky, *The Life of Zabolotsky*, trans. & ed. R. Milner-Gulland (with poems in translation; Univ. of Wales Press, 1994)

D. Goldstein, *Nikolai Zabolotsky: Play for Mortal Stakes* (Cambridge, 1993)

R. Milner-Gulland, 'Zabolotsky: Philosopher-Poet', *Soviet Studies*, April 1971

——, 'Zabolotsky and the Reader: Problems of Approach' (with poems in translation) *Russian Literature Triquarterly* 8 (1974)

F. Björling, *'Stolbcy' by Nikolai Zabolotsky: Analyses* (Stockholm, 1973)

A. Makedonov, *Nikolay Zabolotsky* (Leningrad, 1987)

Vospominaniya o N. Zabolotskom (various memoirs; Moscow, 1984)

A version of the foregoing essay has appeared in N. Cornwall (ed.), *Reference Guide to Russian Literature* (Fitzroy Dearborn, 1998).

Nikolay Alekseyevich Zabolotsky   5

Translator's Preface

Daniel Weissbort

In 1971, I published a small collection of translations of Zabolotsky's poems (Jonathan Cape, Cape Editions). It was entitled *Scrolls*, from Zabolotsky's first collection *Stolbtsy* (1929). This was misleading on two counts: because less than half the contents was from that volume; because *Stolbtsy* can mean either 'Scrolls' or 'Columns' (as in newspaper columns, for instance, though the primary meaning is architectural columns) and it seems more likely that Zabolotsky was leaning towards the latter meaning...

Or was he? Actually, he probably had both meanings in mind. Like many modernists, Nikolay Zabolotsky was also very much of a traditionalist. His translation of the Russian epic, *The Igor Tale*, and his reworking of Russian and Georgian legends testify to his sense of continuity along with his awareness of disjunction. The verse of the *Stolbtsy* period, while it is often jarring and fragmented, surrealistic, absurd (though never nonsensical), grotesquely comical or tragic, is also clearly based on classical models, in particular eighteenth-century philosophic verse. Zabolotsky toys with these models of rational organization and also, as a result, with his readers' expectations. The double significance of the word *Stolbtsy* (Scrolls, Columns), juxtaposing the modern urban world and that of the medieval scribe, is quite apposite.

It was this early poetry of Zabolotsky that attracted me in the first place, to such an extent that I did not readily respond to his superficially more bland post-war (post-Gulag) poetry, although I tried to represent the latter as well in my small selection. While this later poetry still uses modernistic devices and unconventional locutions, it is far less agitated and formally more classical, resisting translation, except insofar as these radical features stand out even more startlingly in such a context than in that of the early poetry (provided, of course, that the translator does not succumb to the temptation to assimilate or conventionalize them). Does this synthesis work? In the Russian, the sheer loveliness of the language gives it a unifying glow. In English translation (inevitably, perhaps) the contrast or shock effect is too stark. My hope, then, is that in a large collection, such as the present one, the whole will inform the parts enough for the latter to acquire some individual life. To sum up, the carnivalesque (Bakhtinian) nature of the early work, linguistically and imagistically rich, lends itself more immediately to translation, while the more finely textured later work tends, in translation, to sound rather romantic, not to say sentimental, this, of course, being no judgement on the poems in Russian, only on my own attempts to translate them into English.

So, I was in a quandary with these later poems of Zabolotsky. The options seemed to be as follows. First, I could render them literally, in a Nabokovian manner. 'The person who desires to turn a literary masterpiece into another language, has only one duty to perform, and this is to reproduce with absolute exactitude the whole text, and nothing but the text', wrote Nabokov in reference to his own translation of Pushkin's *Eugene Onegin*. By 'the whole text' Nabokov meant all the words, together with cultural and historical associations (conveyed, where necessary, in notes as extensive as they needed to be), regardless of 'elegance, euphony, clarity, good taste, modern usage and even grammar', which, he added scornfully, 'the dainty mimic prizes higher than truth'. That Nabokov knew what the truth was went without saying. Another option, even more problematical, was to go into a kind of overdrive and to try to write the same kind of poem in English. My dilemma, with these particular poems, was that there seemed to be no middle way, no negotiating between the two extremes, the loss being so catastrophic that I could not bring myself to settle for either, although my puritanical conscience made me lean towards the first. The fact is that these are poems often ravishingly seductive. I enjoy them more and more and, paradoxically, this has brought me closer to acknowledging my own inability to render them. Nevertheless, a few are included in the present collection (e.g. 'I touched the leaves of the eucalyptus') in the hope that some shadowing forth has occurred, or that the context of a more comprehensive collection of translations, from all periods, will help matters. Still, the volume is necessarily lopsided, in that proportionately less of the later work is to be found in it.

What drew me to *Stolbtsy*, then, was the concreteness

and vigour of Zabolotsky's imagery, of his metaphorical imagination, rather than the richness of the language as such. One reason for this, I dare say, was that at the time, with my relatively limited Russian, I was in any case less capable of appreciating his way with words. Nevertheless, so intensely observed was his world, so visually realized, so painterly, that I responded strongly to it. I had come across his work in the mid-1960s, at a time when I was preoccupied with the 'minimalist' poetry of post-war East Europe. Zabolotsky's work, of course, was quite different, as were the circumstances of its composition; he belonged to an earlier generation and to a less modern, if no less vibrant culture. Still, the precision, the clarity (even in his quite eccentric verse, with its fantasmagoric images, its non-sequiturs or clashes of meaning, its elipticisms), the 'thingness' (*predmetnost*) predisposed me in its favour. Thirty years on, I am still fascinated by Zabolotsky's particularistically visionary work, his materialistic myth-making; but now I am also more responsive to his language. This has made the work of translation both more and less difficult. It is more difficult, because I am now able to analyse it in greater detail; and it is less difficult, because the wholeness, the comprehensiveness of his achievement is now more apparent, and (paradoxically, perhaps) this has given me as translator greater freedom. Of course, I still ask myself whether that freedom has been earned, or whether it is illusory, a temptation that should be resisted...

While my earlier translations were semantically, lexically, as close as I could make them, taking some account of formal considerations, I also tried (in the currently fashionable jargon) to 'domesticate' them, to render them unexceptionably English (the English in question, being of course my own, or that of a middle-class, public-school and Oxbridge-educated Englishman, albeit of Polish Jewish extraction). Just as the above parenthetical qualifications mark the present piece as a product of the politically correct 1990s, so did my translation of the time represent a compromise or accommodation between the prevailing non-literalist ('sense for sense') approach to translation and a somewhat less orthodox literalism. Paradoxically, as I became semantically less literalistic, I became formally and even linguistically more mimetic, although I was not wholly won over by the 'foreignizing' tendency which now appears to be gaining votes among translators, if not among publishers. I have not been able to persuade myself that formal or rhetorical literalism would be appropriate with

Zabolotsky, who insisted on semantic validity and rejected formalism, as such, even if he had learnt much from it. Certainly he himself would not have advocated it. This is on record. But it is not fair either to blame him for the consequences of *my* actions.

So, I have tried to steer a course between the Scylla of domestication and the Charybdis of foreignizing, training myself to be on the lookout for instances where conventionalism had nudged me into toning down images. Wherever I have noticed this happening, sometimes catching myself in the very act, I have tended to restore what had been modified or, in some cases, even discarded. A positive effect of the prolonged gestation of this project, I hope, is that I have learnt to live with what initially had been unacceptable to me. If it cannot be claimed that I have also learnt to trust my reader, I have at least, perhaps, learnt to trust myself a little more. But while I have managed to attenuate Zabolotsky's 'oddness' less than in my earlier translations, I have also found it necessary to write a more normal or standard English, which means that many of the effects Zabolotsky is able to obtain in the Russian (granted, his own normal or standard Russian) have not been nearly as reproducible in English as they might have been had I resorted to a more foreignizing idiom. That is, while I like to think that I have been more attentive to the verbal texture of the original in these later translations than in the earlier ones, semantic considerations still prevail. Zabolotsky is, as I have said, so visual a poet, his vision so literal, that a semantically mimetic approach seems indicated.

Zabolotsky was associated with the 1920s literary group known as OBERIU (The Association of Real Art; see Nikita Zabolotsky and Robin Milner-Gulland in the present volume). A country boy come to the big city and cultural centre of St Petersburg–Petrograd–Leningrad, he joined enthusiastically and with much idealism in the avant-garde artistic life of those difficult and confusing times (radical war communism, followed by Lenin's compromising New Economic Policy). The poems of *Stolbtsy* belong to that period, and are full of contradictions, in that they express both his enjoyment of the carnival, the dissoluteness and what we might call rampant consummerism of the NEP period and also his disillusionment with this outcome of the great events, what amounted to a betrayal of the revolution, even if the revolution he envisaged, involving the liberation of the beasts as well as of humankind, was clearly not that of the Party. (Comparisons, however superficial they may be, with the present situation of conspicuous consumerism, of course, immediately suggest themselves, except that the Party is no longer orchestrating events.) In the heady 1920s, one could still believe in the power of art to affect change.

The OBERIU manifesto, published in January 1928, was largely written by Zabolotsky. The group, which gave cabaret-like dramatic performances and readings and most of whose participants were writers, intended this declaration to be comprehensive, to apply to the fine arts, theatre and cinema, and music, as well as literature. The 'Oberiuti', as they were called, defended the various tendencies of leftist progressive or revolutionary art against those who sought to tame intellectual life and bring it under a single banner, although they also rejected the more radical *zaum* (trans-sense or trans-rational) writers. The latter invented a language that would convey ideas and feelings directly, phonologically, as it were. 'No school', the manifesto emphasized, 'is more hostile to us than zaum.' The *Oberiuti* adhered instead to the notion of materiality, 'thingness'. They tried, in effect, to reconcile utilitarian socialist art (socialist realism) with an art concerned also with its own making. They were looking for a synthesis: *Oberiu*, the manifesto proclaimed hopefully, 'is revolutionary precisely by virtue of this method.'

The manifesto's first section, on poetry, is worth quoting at some length, as it offers clues to Zabolotsky's artistic preoccupations in the formative stage of his career. His position is most clearly evident in the forthrightness with which *zaum* is condemned, since some of the other *Oberiuti* might not have been so adamant in this respect. '[We are] people who are real and concrete to the core', he insists; 'we are the primary enemies of those who castrate the word and turn it into a powerless and senseless mongrel.' This suggests not so much a conventional approach to language as respect for it; if it is worshipped even by time (W.H. Auden), then it is certainly greater than any individual user.

> [...] The concrete object, stripped of its literary and everyday shell, becomes a property of art. In poetry, the clash of verbal meanings expresses this object with the precision of mechanical science. Are you beginning to complain, as it

were, that this is not the same object that you see in life? Come a little closer and feel it with your fingers. Look at the object with your naked eyes and you will see it for the first time stripped of its hoary old literary gilding. Perhaps you will claim that our subjects are 'not real' and 'not logical'? But who said that 'worldly' logic is obligatory for *art*? We are astounded at the beauty of a woman in a painting, regardless of the fact that, contrary to anatomical logic, the artist has dislocated his heroine's shoulder-blade and moved it to one side. Art has its own logic and it does not destroy the object, but allows it to be apprehended.

If language, as received, could achieve this, what need was there to reformulate or re-form it? Following the above are short biographical impressions of each of the poets (A. Vvedensky, K. Vaginov, Igor Bakhterev, N. Zabolotsky, and Daniil Kharms). Zabolotsky describes himself as

> a poet of naked concrete figures, brought right up to the eye of the spectator. One should listen to him and read him more with the eyes and fingers than with the ears. The object does not break up, but on the contrary becomes more integrated and harder, as though preparing to meet the feeling hand of the spectator. The development of the action and the situation are secondary to this main task.

Even under conformist pressure from the Party, a decade later, Zabolotsky hedged when called upon to make a full confession, renouncing his earlier credo. At a plenary session of the Leningrad branch of the Union of Writers, he responded to articles in *Pravda*, attacking Formalism. His speech was published in *Literary Leningrad* on 1 April 1936, under the editorial title: 'The Articles in Pravda Open Our Eyes'. His twists and turns, his attempts to balance the obligatory *mea culpas* with a more measured assessment of his earlier writings make depressing reading. What followed – the arrest, beatings, exile, hard labour – was far worse, but the beginnings were here. If one bears in mind the dedication of Zabolotsky's generation to ideals of humanitarian reform and also the conformism to which they were brutally subjected, the stubborn honesty of the man becomes apparent. In the spirit of self-criticism, he begins:

After *Stolbtsy* was written and the first period of my work was over, it became clear to me that I could not pursue this way any further. The depiction of objects, the elaboration of figures, naturalistic sketches of petty bourgeois life would have been all very well, had the text been illuminated by thought, had all these phenomena been presented in a clear historical perspective. There was hardly any of this in *Stolbtsy*. For me, describing the objects and events of the time was an end in itself. In this lies the formalism of *Stolbtsy*, formalism being a self-sufficient technique, which impoverishes content. Clearly, experimental, formalist tendencies were more apparent in some poems than in others. At that time it seemed to me that one could improve the form independently of content and that these experiments were interesting for their own sake. Of course this was wrong.

He then reasserts the artistic value of his method, the importance of object-centredness. His focus on the phenomenal world bespeaks an appreciation, a love of visual, tactile reality, a sensual responsiveness to the natural environment, meaning that of nature and of man, who is a product of nature. Where the official so-called materialist ideology began with ideas, Zabolotsky, for one, began with materiality.

But *Stolbtsy* taught me to keep the outside world in focus, awoke in me an interest in this, developed the capacity to present phenomena in plastic terms. It let me in on the secret of plastic descriptiveness [...] etc.

'One should listen to him and read him more with the eyes and fingers than with the ears.' This may be an exaggeration, but it is also a striking indication of the importance Zabolotsky attached to concreteness. And it is this particularism, especially in the context of generalities, of the anodyne sentimentalism, characteristic of so much Soviet verse, that impressed me in my initial encounters with this great poet, whose early work was being rediscovered, at the time, in Russia itself. I suppose that, although in my naïvety I thought I was being guided primarily by aesthetic considerations, I was also responding to political and social changes occurring behind the Iron Curtain after Stalin's death, that found expression in the arts, especially in poetry. My part, like that of others more aware of what was going on, was of course an unheroic one, but not without relevance in the struggle against totalitarianism. Faced with the classical dilemma as to whether, practically speaking, freedom could or should precede the quest for social justice, the translator might conclude that, if not freedom, then at least non-totalitarianism was a legitimate aim. In certain historical situations, translators, in spite of their shrinking nature, can sometimes find themselves in the role of message-bearers, preservers of key texts, broadcasters – to whatever section of humanity is disposed to listen – of words that tyrannical regimes or individuals have attempted to suppress. And so, under the impulse of this double (aesthetic and socio-political) imperative, I probably felt that it was not necessarily so presumptuous of me to try to translate Zabolotsky's verse.

Later, much later, when I got to know a little about some of the painters who influenced Zabolotsky, particularly Pavel Filonov, the visual acuity of the poems, and their painterly-compositional qualities, became still more apparent, this reinforcing my impression. The OBERIU manifesto's note on Zabolotsky tends to support these initial intuitions. At the same time, while much of the experimental work of the early years of the century now seems of little more than documentary interest, Zabolotsky managed to draw what he needed from the radical notions in the air. That is to say, he was not simply carried away by them, even though the story is complicated by the fact that he lived through the Stalinist purges and survived a period in the camps, in the Far East, 1938–44, so that his revisions of earlier work and his formally more serene later work, bringing him more into line apparently with the official aesthetics, might be taken as a surrender to pressure. And, indeed, it would have been surprising if his artistic development had not to some extent been distorted by events. But there is more to it than that. For whatever reason – and his village origins no doubt played a part – he never lost touch with the natural world, nor with the history of humankind and its relation to that natural world. One of Zabolotsky's sources may have been Engels's *Dialectics of Nature*, but his nature-philosophy was not limited by a dialectical materialist interpretation of the world.

It is possible that had I not visited Joseph Brodsky in New York, in December 1995, a month or so before his death, I would never have let go of these translations. Not, of course, that he should be blamed for my having done so...

For whatever reason, I had never quite believed that Brodsky liked Zabolotsky's work, although he assured me that he did, that he regarded him as among the greatest poets, perhaps the greatest, of the Soviet period. (As Nikita Zabolotsky points out in his memoir, Akhmatova, Mandelshtam, Pasternak, Tsvetayeva belonged, in a sense, to the pre-Soviet period.) Indeed, it was almost as though this went without saying, which is perhaps why I could not at first hear it, thinking that Brodsky was simply being nice, or trying to encourage me, since obviously I was going to continue translating the man anyway. Gradually it dawned on me that Zabolotsky was, if not everybody's, then certainly a surprising number of writers' favourite poet. At the same time, he is hugely popular, and it is surely no accident that the print-run of the last Soviet edition (1989) of the work of a poet who was banned during most of his creative life was one million copies.

It is true that Brodsky intimated to me that he greatly preferred the somewhat neglected late, more 'classical' Zabolotsky to the early avantgardist. However, this did not mean that he rejected the early work. On the contrary, as is clear from the recently published conversations with Volkov, he regarded *Columns* and 'Agriculture Triumphant' as representing an exceedingly important stage in the development of Russian poetry of the twentieth century. Of course, Brodsky was talking from within the language and its poetic development, whereas I was looking at Zabolotsky's work through the prism of translation, translatability, and the literary context of my own language.

It occurs to me now that Brodsky's affinity for Zabolotsky, although he never wrote about him, may have had something to do with his (Brodsky's) almost preternatural sensitivity to spatial relationships. Though Brodsky's bond with the objects of his world was more metaphysical than Zabolotsky's, there is nevertheless a certain similarity in their preoccupations. At any rate, when I sat down with Brodsky and we spent several hours mulling over the opening section (24 lines) of Zabolotsky's long poem, 'Agriculture Triumphant' (it was Brodsky's idea to give it this title in English, rather than the more obvious 'The Triumph of Agriculture'), it became obvious that he was not simply paying lip service to a respected and respectable Russian poet's memory, but that he understood and loved him. Perhaps a few words, then, about our all too brief collaboration on this poem, a poem which Zabolotsky had hoped would be acceptable to the Party idealogues but which was treated as a slander on collectivization and contributed to his imprisonment and exile.

The fact is that Zabolotsky had not compromised his fundamental belief in a revolution that would embrace all living creatures, his anthropocentrism being decidedly unorthodox. His visionary and idealistic poem did not meet with a favourable reception, not only because the Party's notion of the Revolution was quite different, but also because the absurdist manner of his early work had not been sufficiently toned down. In 1936, in the speech before a plenary session of the Leningrad branch of the Writers' Union quoted earlier, Zabolotsky tried to explain his motivation for writing 'The Triumph':

> In 1929, at the very start of the collectivisation process, I decided to write my first long poem, dedicating it to those great events that were taking place around me. [...] You remember Velemir Khlebnikov's lines: 'What I see is freedom for horses / And equal rights for cows...' I was much taken with them. [...] A time is approaching when, as Engels puts it, people will not only feel, but also be conscious of their unity with nature [...] The new man of the classless society, having replaced predatory exploitation by universal creative labour and planning, must in future extend this principle to his relationship with nature in its enslaved state. A time will come, therefore, when Man the exploiter will turn into Man the organizer of nature... [...]

Nevertheless, the subject of the poem and its conclusion (however unorthodox the treatment and the ruralist or ecological vision of a comprehensive 'revolution'), Zabolotsky's attempt to placate the regime, was unlikely to appeal to Brodsky, I thought, although we did not spend much time discussing the political aspects of Zabolotsky's poetry. (Actually, both Zabolotsky and Brodsky were essentially apolitical, even if the latter, in the later part of his American 'incarnation', was inclined to make political pronouncements or even to write on political topics. It seemed to me, though, that this was more an indication of the comparatively low regard in which he held politics and politicians.) In any case, evidently Brodsky was not put off. Zabolotsky was a great poet, with a historical and cosmic vision very much of its time but not irrelevant to ours, who did the best he could, under dire circumstances. Brodsky was never an apologist for capitalism (or for any other ism), notwithstanding the various pressures and encouragements to fulfil his prescribed role as a Soviet exile, nor was he interested in condemning others less fortunate than himself.

So, after the many discussions, extending over two decades, all we had time to actually work on together was the prologue to 'Agriculture Triumphant'. Still, this passage was one I had despaired of rendering convincingly, my most recent version resorting somewhat fraudulently to a kind of impacted diction which I hoped might at least avoid losing the reader right away. As Brodsky pointed out, Zabolotsky employs classical metres only to subvert them. This is particularly evident in these opening lines. The resulting metrical unease reflects uncertainties in this opening passage that conflict with the optimism suggested by the poem's title. Darra Goldstein (*Nikolai Zabolotsky: Play for Mortal Stakes*, 1993) comments on Zabolotsky's anachronistic juxtaposition of different traditions, folk-verse and epic. This macaronic tendency, too, might have appealed to Brodsky, whose own poetry often represents an eclectic mixture of styles and traditions.

Brodsky sprawled on the floor, like a child with its toys, while I hovered, uncomfortably adult, in an armchair. It was as if he were holding the Russian poem in one hand, while he jostled bunches of English words in the other. He seemed literally to be weighing the two groups of words, trying to balance them. And, indeed, what he said to me was: 'Your translation is not sprightly enough!' That is, the teeming infelicities of the version appeared not to concern him nearly so much as the failure to sense or to realize the metrical buoyancy of Zabolotsky's Russian. What he had his eye, his ear, or his finger on, in particular, was the rhythm. It would not have occurred to me, even on an experimental basis, to take such liberty with wording and even sense (at least locally) for the sake of metre. Brodsky's approach was metrically literalistic, as Nabokov's was semantically so. But, different as these two approaches seem to be, they also resemble one another in that the source text, the Russian, is allowed to infiltrate or foreignize the English.

Of course, Brodsky addressed the text, as a Russian poet, almost as though it were one he had composed himself. He heard it, firstly, from the inside, as sound and rhythm, abstractly, one might say. This, in short, was where the process began; the structure or framework had to be established, since without it the poem was simply a gabble of words, a guide to content and no more. As for the content, in the largest sense, Brodsky could deploy his profound knowledge and acute intuitions, even if his ear for the English sometimes let him down. He was, in short, in a privileged position as a translator, and his advice had to be treated with some caution. Nevertheless, the *physicality* of his approach was inspiring. It left nothing essential outside the translator's purview, making him feel less of a compromiser than usual. Loss was, of course, entailed but at least this did not come about for want of trying!

I scribbled notes as Brodsky improvised, trying with his English to represent the bounce of the original, not bothering much about being idiomatic, or about the correct use of definite and indefinite articles and so forth, but along the way chancing on rhymes that pleased, encouraged or amused him. In fact, he became quite animated, getting up and walking around the room; as ·his mind engaged with the poem, so did his body.

He made another comment. When translating Zabolotsky's verse, if in doubt, always opt for the more absurd solution! This was liberating. The fact is one needs all the ingenuity one can muster when translating Zabolotsky, and Brodsky's remark seemed to release my own ingenuity, such as it is. Is this just a round-about way of justifying having taken more liberties with the literal text than I might have been inclined to do otherwise? I suppose it is. At the same time, though, I find myself advancing the time-worn claim that one has to be free or daring in order to be faithful or remain close. If Zabolotsky was daring, could a timid translator hope to emulate him? On the other hand, is emulation called for? The translator's classical dilemma! I remain doubtful about the 'liberties', although I continue to hope that, after thirty years, one can afford to take a few.

If the above is making the reader rather uneasy, let me reassure him or her that these *are* translations and not imitations, or my own poems.

Approximately a third of all Zabolotsky's short poems are included, and all four of his long ones. While I have translated nearly all of his poems, I decided not to include those which, for whatever reason, linguistic or contextual, were particularly refractory. Unfortunately, many of these, as indicated above, were also among his most beautiful late poems. While over half the pre-war poems are included, fewer than a fifth of the post-war ones are. I have made an exception with *Stolbtsy* (Columns), Zabolotsky's sensational first book, the whole of which is included here, even though I am dubious about some of the poems in my English version. With *Stolbtsy*, as with all the early poems, I have translated from the original texts, rather than the revised versions. Too many of the revisions appear to have been influenced by non-aesthetic considerations, even if some seem to me to be improvements. I felt that the least problematical procedure was simply to present the texts as they first appeared.

In a later edition of this collection, if there is one, I may include the variants, along with the entire poetic oeuvre. Nikita Zabolotsky, the poet's son and author of *The Life of Zabolotsky* (edited and translated by Robin Milner-Gulland, 1994), in an act of extraordinary filial devotion has also assembled a volume of Zabolotsky's entire poetic work, with biographical and textual commentary, a selection of the letters, translations and prose, documents, photographs, and memoirs and critical comments by contemporaries. Entitled *Ogon' mertsayushchii v sosude* (Moscow, 1995; 'Flame Flickering in the Vessel', from a late poem, 'The Ugly Girl', not included in the present collection) this volume presents the material in seven sections: Childhood, Youth, Student Days (1903–25); Early Maturity (1926–9; this includes *Stolbtsy*); The Thirties in Leningrad (1930–7); Prison and Camp (1938–44; only two poems, mostly letters); Return to Poetry (1945–8); In Moscow (1948–56); Late Hopes (1956–8). These divisions make good sense with a virtually complete text, but in the present volume I have reduced the number of divisions. I have distinguished between *Columns* and 'Pre-imprisonment Poems' not because they are necessarily different in kind, but because *Columns* is the only 'book' I include *in toto*. Although he was permitted to publish very few books, Zabolotsky assembled them very carefully. *Columns* is also, of course, the collection that brought the poet to the notice of Russian readers. I have grouped the 'Long Poems', all written in the 1930s, and I have one final section, 'Post-imprisonment Poems', along with which I have included the two poems directly relating to his Gulag experience, even though they were written during the war.

As for the translations themselves, I have not, for instance, sought to rhyme wherever the original does. It seemed folly to try to impose that kind of consistency. With *Columns*, since the whole collection is to be found here, I have aimed at greater formal imitation. Otherwise, Zabolotsky's descriptiveness called, I thought, for sharpness of wording as much as it did for formal mimesis. So, if I have aimed at a kind of unity it is, perhaps, one of descriptive effect. With the later poems, classically restrained, no longer playing with traditional forms but simply adhering to them, paradoxically I found myself unable or unwilling to follow suit. Instead, I used lines of variable length and tried to achieve tonal consistency. The problem, of course, is that stripped of their traditional form and imagistically restrained, these poems tend to sound all too prosaic. Nevertheless, my sense was that what they required (at least of me) was semantic fidelity. I know that this seems to contradict the imperatives noted with regard to the earlier poems, but I cannot help that. William Merwin once wrote that each poem he translates presents him with a new challenge and new problems, whether by the same author or not. I tend to agree with that, even though it upsets me and I have also done the best I can, in the present volume, to convey Zabolotsky's wholeness of vision.

It only remains for me to express my appreciation for the help and encouragement I have received over the decades. In particular I should like thank Robin Milner-Gulland, the leading Zabolotsky scholar in the West, a number of whose fine translations are included in this book. He was always ready to answer my neophyte questions and has continued to support my endeavours. I am also deeply grateful to Nikita Zabolotsky and his wife Natasha, with whom I stayed in Moscow, working at Nikolai Zabolotsky's desk and among his archives. Ted Hughes sought to boost my frail translator's ego and urged me to get this collection out. Joseph Brodsky, with whose views on translation I often disagreed, though it became clear to me later that we were talking about different things, in the end made the observations that might have set me back on my heels, but which also supplied the catalyst needed for me to complete this work. Finally, there are my several dear ones... But it seems pretentious to talk of them, as if what I have accomplished were of such moment that a thank-offering was called for. I don't think translation is like that. Naturally, I alone must take responsibility for the versions as here presented.

Columns

THE RED BAVARIA[1]

In the depths of a bottle paradise,
whose palm-trees long ago dried up,
playing beneath electric lights,
a window floated in a cup;
it glittered with the turning blades,
then sank down under its own weight;
above it beery vapour curled...
But how to describe such a world.

And in that bottle paradise
sirens shivered on the apron
of the crooked stage. Their eyes,
were issued to them on probation.
Enamelled arms reached for the skies,
they munched on sandwiches to hide
their tedium, distraught and jaded.

On tenterhooks, the doors spin round,
tumbling down the steps, a crowd,
cardboard dickeys crackling,
embottled, dancing in a ring;
behind the bar, a siren pales,
with booze the customers regales;
she comes and goes, looking askance,
guitar in hand, stands apart,
sings about her love, how she
brought her beloved lots to eat,
how tender and cruelly
the silk lace bit into her body,
how whiskey hung there in the glasses,
and how, with temple blasted,
splattering his breast with blood,
suddenly he fell. O, broken heart!
And all she sang about that night,
in the glass, was shot with white.

The men as well kept up the rumpus,
staggering from pew to pew,
on the ceiling, set askew

a mirrored bedlam, halves with flowers;
one of them bites off his tongue,
another yells: I'm Christ, so come
and worship, for I am your saviour,
nails in my armpits and all over...
A siren approaches, with a lurch,
and now, a knee bestraddled,
the conclave of glasses, rabid, addled,
sparks like a chandelier in church.

Eyes, like lead, plummetted,
cracking a goblet – night drew up,
and with it, greasy cars,
tucking Piccadilly[2] under their arm,
took off smoothly.
In the cool, tomatoes grew,
and now the Red Bavarian suns
let themselves down, settling anew
onto the bottom of the casks,
while outside, amid wintery blasts,
a lantern glittered on a mast.

There the Nevsky, shiny, bored,
having switched skins overnight,
its praises sung by sleepy horns,
troubled the Red Bavaria's sign,
and through the fog, the crowd, the fumes,
to the Hermandad's policing whistles,[3]
above the tower a winged globe zooms,
holding aloft the name of 'Singer'.[4]

[August 1926]

1. Red Bavaria was Zabolotsky's first published work, in the 1927 Union of Leningrad
    Poets' collection *Bonfire*. The Red Bavaria was a drinking establishment in
    Leningrad, in the 1920s, close by the *Dom Knigi* (House of the Book). The ceiling
    was covered with glass panes.
2. Piccadilly. Old name of a cinema on the Nevsky Prospekt, later called The Aurora.
3. Hermandad, [Spanish/brotherhood]. In Spain, originally a league against the
    oppression of the nobles; a voluntary organization that afterwards turned into the
    regular police force.
4. 'Singer' is the sewing-machine firm. Its name appeared on the globe over the dome
    of the building on the corner of Nevsky and the Griboedov Canal. Later this building
    became The House of the Book.

WHITE NIGHT

Look! No ball, no masquerade,
evenings follow, out of phase,
parrotlike, from mouth to mouth,
drunken laughter loops, uncouth;
bridges and bluffs have split in two,
lovers race by in a crowd;
one burns up, another droops,
and a third is quite fagged out...
Love moans underneath the leaves,
restlessly changes places, heaves,
backs off and then draws near...
But the muses are in love all year.

The Nevka's waters pitched and slapped
at the rails, a drum began
to rattle, while in a crescent,
rockets ascended in succession.
After these spiralled fiery pears,
like bellies whirling in the skies.

In the trees, rings rocked and pitched,
smoke, in clotted tatters, dripped
from torches. But on the Nevka,
sirens or simply wenches –
sirens, most likely – rose,
silvery-blue from head to toe,
cold, and yet pale as straw
their lips, motionlesss like medals,
calling out to be kissed, all
of this nothing but pretence.

And I walked on. The night
sprawled across the grass, chalk-white:
over it bushes stood perpendicularly,
sheathed in iridescent steel,
and nightingales, on a twig above,
bleakly cuckooed. From their ditty,
they seemed to be experiencing pity –
they had no aptitude for love.

And there, inflating, like an angel,
lying in wait for holy saints,
squatting Yelagin Island rose,
swilled, rinsed and then fell silent:
this time two lovers were exposed.

With turning screws, a steamer,
langorous melodies on board,
comes, boats trundle out to meet her,
nothing in the rowers' heads;
she nudges them and they are off,
running, running, then once more
coming her way... 'You fools!'
she howls: 'I'll cripple you!'
But they are convinced she'll not...

It's pandemonium all about,
the white air clinging to the gables,
and night's got one foot in the grave now,
rocking up and down on scales,
So, the premature babe or angel,
opening its milky eyes,
rocks in a jar of alcohol,
and craves a favour of the skies.

[July 1926]

SOCCER

Exultantly the forward runs,
now what's it got to do with him!
It is as if his bones upheld
his body splitting at the seams.
His soul flows cloaklike in the wind,
his clavicle resounds against
where this cloak is taken in.
The membrane in his ear vibrates,
while grapes dance in his throat –
that spheroid thing o'erflies the row.

They close in on him, make a grab,
they offer him a poisoned snack,
but far more terrible than that
is their heels' arsenic.
Back!
The backs have piled up in a heap,
billowing from the draught,
but over ocean, sea, and stream,
over square and snowy waste,
setting its splendid armour straight,
into its meridian
lists the ball.

Exultantly, the forward falls
upon the flames, unscrews his knees,
but a fount's already gushing
from his throat, he pitches, screams:
'Treachery!' The ball, walled, spinning through,
smokes, swells, laughs out loud,
shuts an eye down tight, then shouts:
'Night!' Then opens: 'How d'y do!'
It's torturing the lad, no doubt.

One goal, two goals, three goals, four,
no trumpet blast to sound the score,
the melancholic goalkeeper
keeps track, wiping the slate clean,
and calls for night. The night draws near,
clanking its diamantine door;
it inserts a pitch-black key
into the atmosphere's cavity:
A hospital! Alas the day!
Headless, the forward slips away.

Above him is a stubborn globe,
two lances pierce it, cruciform,
graveyard water from the slab
trickles into shallow grooves,
in his throat the grapes dry up.
Sleep, forward, back to front!

Sleep, poor forward!
Overhead,
darkly night starts its descent,
maids are dancing in the glow
with the pale-blue stream below;
in the little lilac house,
the wallpaper is fading fast,
mother ages day by day...
Sleep, poor forward!
We're away.

[August 1926]

THE SEA

Mounts of antiquity arose,
war broke out and boulders tore,
screaming, above battling hordes,
encircled by an eerie glow.
The sea blackened about the boat,
and the waves that lay across its road
chattered like heaps of silver spoons.
Like blind drags, gleaming at its side,
they raved, and from their jaws,
their black jaws, joyfully
gushed a stream of molten glass,
flowed and fell, and swelled,
then swayed, spattered, fell again.
A great wave rose to meet it then,
and the storm whirled in a manic waltz,
yelling at the boat: 'You're caught!'
screaming: 'Got you! Got you!' Or:
'Dump all your cargo overboard!'

Unmanned or for the fun of it,
the searchlight pressed upon the waves,
and like stone women, monoliths,
they were blinded. The wind treated
the flag more circumspectly,

and the flag crackled like paper
ripped. The storm
subsided and finally the moon came out,
slipping its shine between decks,
and the damp lustre searched for warmth
by the stacks' heat. A flush
spread across the waves, stumbling green,
lips mumbling at the stern...

[November 1926]

AN ETCHING

And it thundered all round the dumbstruck hall:
'The deceased's on the run from the royal home!'

The deceased proudly strolls through the town,
by the bridle the lodgers are leading him on,
with trumpetlike voice a prayer he intones,
and he's wringing his hands.
He sports copper specs with membraneous frames,
subterranean water's filled him to the brim,
above, wooden birds on the shutters
close their wings with a clump.
All around, a crashing, a clanging of cylinders
and a sky, curly-headed, while here –
a small urban box with an unfastened door
and behind the glass pane, rosemary.

[January 1927]

THE CIRCASSIAN GIRL

When dawn, a transparent density,
squeezes the air above the ground,
eagles, twin planes converging,
fly from the bell-resembling mount.
Trees enter, multi-faceted,
their magical, nomad encampment.
The summit smoulders like a candle;
adorned with metal rings, it jangles.
But there, beyond and far above,
nodding his splendid heights,
old man Elbrus offers us
a cup of tea and turkish delight.

Then suddenly the Caucasus,
a five-nippled hulk, sails forth,
like a boat with festoons hung
into Leningrad's splendid warp,
and the Circassian girl, before
a rainbow shop window droons;
for her, Tula[1] a foxtrot forged,
Tambov[2] is fitting her for shoes,
but Terek,[3] surging in her breast,
breaks through the lacerated lips –
she falls corpselike, her arms
folded, triangular and neat.

The Neva flows like the Aragva,[4]
but to the stars all honour,
for they have laid a wreath of lead
upon the limey, little dead,
and so she 'sleeps'... Forgive her God!
Over her body garlands nod,
and drifting athwart the watery race,
the Putilov[5] moon its progress makes.

And I stand there – white from the light.
I gaze into the pitchy sea,
and the world before my eyes divides
into two gigantic boots.

One of them is planted on Elbrus,[6]
the other one is talking Finnish,
and both together they make off,
thundering eastward across the seas.

[January 1926]

1. Tula was known for gramophones and samovars.
2. There were shoe factories in Tambov (*Tambovskie sapozhki*).
3. The Terek is a river flowing from the Caucasian Range into the Caspian Sea.
4. The Aragva is a mountain river flowing from the Caucasian Range into the River Kura.
5. Putilov: the largest industrial complex in Leningrad, later the Kirov works, concentrating on machine-building and metallurgy.
6. Elbrus is the highest peak in the Caucasus (Georgia).

SUMMER

The crimson sun was suspended lengthwise,
and I wasn't the only one who was cheerful –
the bodies of people grew juicy as pears,
and their little heads nodded, ripening on top.
The trees turned flabby. The trees turned to fat,
like tallow candles. And it seemed to us that
it wasn't a dusty stream flowing past,
but a plug of sputum pulled out till it burst.
And night arrived. In these glorious meadows,
prickly stars caught like burs in the flowers,
like balls, fleecy sheep lay about,
the trees, those curly-topped tapers, went out.
A foot-soldier shepherd, ensconced in a gully,
drew a diagram of the moon,
and dogs fought over their cross-roads, disputing
which one of them was to stand guard.

[August 1927]

THE SENTRY

On guard, the night grows darker,
the sentry, like a puppet, stands,
in his sightless eyes there hovers
the tetrahedal bayonet.
Like icon-lamps, before him hang
splendid regimental banners,
suspended from the ceiling with
their sickles crumpled and their hammers.
A proletarian on a horse
roars in the moonlight and cavorts;
the regimental cuckoo's howl
glumly sinks behind the wall;
and a small white house appears,
with a square turret set on top,
and on its ramparts sways a maid,
tooting a translucent horn.
Already cows are hastening to her,
with pallid smiles upon their lips...
But in the dark the sentry stands,
wrapped in his conical greatcoat;
above him, a stellar conflagration,
the sacred sickle crowns his bed.
Now, between interstices
of flagstones, mouse visages peek,
like little triangles of chalk,
with sorrowing eyes on either side...
One of these perches in the window,
a floret of music in its hand,
and the day extends its fingers through
the grille, but cannot reach the flags.
It makes a further effort, sees
the sentry, like a puppet, standing,
and the proletarian on a horse
protects him, straightening the lances.
Hanging banners are his bedhead
and the bayonet's a call to war...
And the day approves him more and more.

[February 1927]

THE NEW LIFE

The sun emerges over Moscow,
old women run about in sorrow;
where, oh where shall we go now?
The New Life's knocking at the door!
The babe is whittled smooth, it seems,
seated like a pasha in the font;
a priest moans like a tambourine,
chandelier-lit and radiant;
great-grandma's snuffing out the candle,
the infant is approaching manhood,
but the New Life's mounted on a steed,
while the babe proceeds on hands and knees.
It doesn't hurt, he is not vexed,
brownish, star-shaped patch on patch
is fastened to his modest breast –
for him there is no going back.
Already he looks down from on high
(a fine-grained whetstone in each eye),
then feasts until he can no more,
as the great working day unfurls;
look, the babe is swilling beer,
he's got his hands on boozy girls,
and striding across the table tops,
into the Komsomol[1] he plops!

But the season shrivels, yellow-hued,
daddy is growing old as well,
and outside on the avenue,
the matchmaker strokes her little bells.
Now the infant's soles have widened,
his forearm's thickened from the steel,
already he's got a large apartment
and holds his bride fast by the sleeve.
A priest strides on, with swinging limbs,
relics nestling in his palm,
his object is to bless this house,
to give the bride a crucifix...
The infant says: 'Be off, priest, scram!'
shoves him: 'Beat it, hairy knave!

I'm the New Life's militiaman,
and all that awaits *you* is the grave!'
The priest is on the verge of tears,
stands and mutters on the stairs,
then steals off, weeping banefully;
the babe guffaws and nods his head,
whispers to his bride: 'That ninny! –
Wait till I get you into bed!'

But now the factories howl, Hooray!
and there appear familiar faces;
serving sturgeon on a plate,
the New Life is dispensing graces.
Preserves, uplifted on a spoon,
have managed to turn fresh again,
unbearably adroit, the groom
clings to his fiancée like a snake;
staggering, the chairman sings
the praises of the happy couple,
and in a Vyborg² goblet brings
soldier's wine and with it halva,
while acknowledging this fine oration,
Ilyich³ is squatting on the table.

'Hurrah! Hurrah!' the factory howls,
like spuds smoke lifts into the air,
and now the happy couple lolls –
and see, they're combing out their hair!
And everything is right on track;
the night arrives and then goes back,
while outside the window, in a trice,
the ecclesiastic lamplight dies.

[1927]

1. Komsomol. Young Communist League.
2. Zabolotsky did his military service in the Vyborg region.
3. In Soviet editions of this poem, the reference to 'Ilyich', Lenin, was suppressed;
   kulich (Easter cake) was substituted.

MOVEMENT

Seated on his throne, the coachman,
his armour wadding, breast to loin,
and his beaver, like an icon's,
lies there, jingling with coins.
And the poor nag's limbs are wagging,
stretching like a coney-fish,
with, again, its eight legs flashing
in its belly, all aglow.

[December 1927]

AT THE MARKET

Decked with flowers, hung with pots,
the market's opened wide its gates.

Women here are stout as wine-casks,
in shawls incomparably fine,
and pickled cucumbers, like tritons,
assidulously tread the brine.
Like sabres herrings flash,
their beady little eyes unbrash,
but split the beggars with a knife,
like limber snakes they roll up tight;
by courtesy of the mighty axe,
meat slumps like a red orifice,
and a sausage, like a bloody gut,
in a clumsy brazier scuds;
following it, a wiry cur
points his lean muzzle in the air,
his mouth gaping like a door,
and his head like a dish,
his legs keeping accurate time,
bending slowly in the middle.
But with a pitiful expression –
What's up! –
he's stopped and a grape-like tear
flies through the laden atmosphere.

The maimed are strung out in a row,
one of them strums a guitar;
he leans back as far as he can go,
lending him a hand, his stump,
to which, to keep him up to scratch,
a peg-leg bottle is attached.
His embryonic arm another
brags about and flourishes,
sticks a finger in his mouth and tweaks,
and like a mole the finger squeaks,
cracking as the bones intersect –
and his face knits itself into a thimble next.

A third one, twirling his moustache,
stares like a hero of the wars,
in his squinting tartarish eyes,
neither anxiety nor repose;
his carriage is a thwart on wheels,
his mouth conceals the sturdy helm,
somewhere in a grave his arms
are withering, while in some stream
his legs sleep... All that now is left
this hero is a paunch and head
and a large mouth, like a shaft,
by which to steer the merry craft.

A wall-eyed granny, over there,
sits on a solitary chair,
and a little book with magic pinpricks
(her fingers' sweet companion)
sings officials at their pulpits,
the woman's fingers scampering...

She dreams of a dog,
and one's supplied
by the meticulous hand of fate;
it stands before her, quite beside
itself, by its lovely soul oppressed!
Around it, like Magellans, weights,
scraps of butter, sweat of love,
freaks like graven images

with rich, calculating blood,
and the yelp of the suppliant guitar,
and hats aglitter, like tiaras,
with brass and copper...

Soon, in their shaky den encased,
both of them – he, drunk, red-faced
from the cold, the stump, the booze,
armless, plump – she, blind to boot,
a hag – will sweetly dance
the lovely Capricorn, so that
the rafters begin to sag and crack
and sparks are kicked up by their heels...
Like a mouse, the old lamp squeals.

[December 1927]

FEAST

In the iron, army chamber,
where the pyramid of rifles sleeps,
the coppery growl of constellations
resounds, the horses' measured beat.
It flies along, my cart, my waggon,
thundering on quadrangle wheels,
and in the wagon, in their spiked
helmets, noisy heroes ride.
A rattling gun, like fingers tapping,
while the suckling bullets squirm;
a battle-cry, a fearful racket,
the enemy is overturned.
But the horse streaks through the air,
its body drawn out, fore and aft,
with its sharp legs severing
the level prison-cell of shafts.

Chiselled flowers cause a stir,
fingers squeezing gather heat,
and night stands us a cask of beer,

a keg of of toasts and tons of speech.
With a stony, goblet rumble,
in the coppery, beery flow,
we drink a camp of tumblers,
with bayonets drawn, all set to go.
We drink and locks of hair vibrate,
steam rising from our sweaty hands,
but faces flattened out like plates,
and the small flame of the lamp
in a blue flow, falls away,
settling on the darkling palm;
like gaffs, the flags are raised,
and impressed into the letters are
a flame, the rifles' harelike laughter,
innuendos, quarrelling rafters,
and through the shredded, riven mist,
a cup by a bayonet transfixed!

O, bayonet, flying everywhere,
cold as a corpse and bloody too,
stab him again and I will lin on
O, bayonet, running Judas through!
I see you floating in the mists,
your flattened edges coming clear,
I see you sail the watery wastes,
a snub-nosed, tetrahedral spear.
Where, earlier, a smoky god
swirled and the world lit candles to him;
where flocks of printed angels held
the sky, and trailed behind them
empty, good-for-nothing wings –
radiant as an incubus,
there you tear along, redeeming
all of these vain delusions.[1]

But that is not what you are after,
and this is not the flight for you –
the infantry across the water
spreads, across the waters you turn too.
Across the water spread contingents –
in my coat, I'm standing there,

only a few weeks old, an infant,
with a soldier's wall-eyed stare.
I've dug out my tobacco pouch,
an empty, unlit pipe retrieved,
while like kids the bullets scout,
gazing longingly at me.

[January 1928]

1. The Russian text here has Kashchei, a folklore character, a skinny, old immortal,
who traps travellers.

THE IVANOVS

The trees stand straight, like nosy clerks,
looking in on you and me,
long ago their nomad life
ended, railed in now, under lock and key.
Constricted boulevards protest,
by seried houses sorely pressed.

Now all the doors are opened wide,
a whispered rumour's gone the rounds:
the Ivanov boys have hit their stride,
in shoes and trousers, office-bound.
Sleek, empty tram-cars tempt them with
vacant benches. Clambering
on board, our heroes buy
brittle pasteboard tickets, sit
and stare at them with neutral eyes
the tram's speed does not galvanize.

The world by bland façades is squeezed,
standing before us like the seas;
amid the thundering asphalt waves,
dart siren maidens, here and there
flickering between the blades
of wheels, in clouds of orange hair.
Others, dressed like simple sallies,
won't just cool their heels at home;

with nimble feet transcribing ballets,
they trip along: 'Where shall I go,
to whose ears press my blood-red lips,
murmur "pet", and by whose bed
drop a bootie, loose a bow?
There must be somewhere I can go!'

World, oh leaden idol, hose
them down, and may your expansive waves
bring these baggages repose,
at the crossroads, head over heels!
The terrible world's asleep tonight;
on the home front, peace and quiet.

So, am I really to be placed
there where a fiancée awaits,
where, in a row, chairs stand up straight,
where a cabinet, in doilies draped,
rises like Ararat, and where
a table's set and a samovar
huffs like a home-brewed general,
three-tiered and clad in armour-plate!

O, world, curl up into a ball,
a city block, a potholed road,
a single, filthy warehouse, all
besmeared, a mouse's hole,
but be prepared to go to war:
Ivanóv has kissed his whore!

[January 1928]

The first title of this poem was 'Street Reflections'. Ivanov, of course, is a very common
Russian surname, like Smith.

WEDDING

A long ray streaks between the logs,
the mighty house stands in the darkness,
a scorching fire reaches out
through windows in their stony bodice.
Medallions, like brass insignia, dangle,
a deserted lamp is driven frantic
over a number, gouged out by
the wretched lodger in the attic.
And down wide corridors, in which
beams clamber to the ceiling,
where a domestic rat has breached
a human burrow for himself –
the kitchen seems to us an organ,
with its hundred-pipe palaver,
sparkling like a bulbous faucet,
performing on the wedding salver.
We hear the noisy play, the grind
of coffee-mills, turning in the wind,
see-sawing in the dark,
four-sided, elegant, and stark,
while, a toast-master, on the flames,
the squatting frying-pan declaims.

Like the black sun of granaries,
the queen of mines loaded with spoils,
it's sliced two lobsters into strips,
anointed with the cooking oils!
It's recognized the coquetry
of fried eggs as the heart of being;
over it a chicken, scrubbed
black and blue, reviles its childhood.
The chicken's closed its baby eyes,
has knit its many-coloured brow,
and in an earthen table-coffin
has laid its sleepy body down.
Over it no priest has brayed
mass, brandishing a crucifix,
no more does the cuckoo serenade it
with its crafty little ditty.

To the belling of cabbages it's chained,
and in tomato vestments clad,
upon it slim-limbed celery
like a little cross is laid.
So in its prime it's shuffled off
this mortal coil, a wretched dwarf.

The clock chimes. It is night.
The banquet's hot and passionate.
The heavy goblet can't set right
the fiery curve of occiput.
An ample flock of fleshy women
sits around, in feathered sheen,
bosoms wreathed in threadbare ermine,
shiny with sweat, centennial queens.
They gorge on cloying sweetmeats,
in unrequited passion wheeze,
and letting out their bellies, cosy
up to bouqets and crockery.
Their husbands, balding and erect,
are seated there like gunshots, yet
the fortress of their collar kneeds
the neck until it's raw and bleeds,
and on the table wine cavorts,
meat, in trenchloads, stretching out,
while in this apoplectic vista,
this bland array of stuck-up snouts,
like some sweet utopic vision,
ethics on little pinions floats.

O, carefree creature, where's your shame?
And what does it profit you, O groom,
tightly hitched to your betrothed,
forgotten now the beat of hooves?
It still retains, your mobile visage,
traces of the wedding garland;
the ring upon the youthful digit
glitters like a desperado;
and the priest, that nightly witness, parts
his whiskers, lifts them like a visor,
a large guitar across his shoulder,
towering above the dance.

Strike up, guitar! Circle, spread out!
The heavy goblets caterwaul.
But the priest shivers, gives a howl,
and briskly thumps the golden cords!
The last glass plummets to the ground,
and ended is the awful dinner,
and now the dancing whirls the crowd,
like zombies, through an open mirror.
It waves its convoluted arms,
and like a coffee mill it spins,
across its face it runs its palms,
and then it cries: Come on! Come on!
Well then, come on!
Not to be outsmarted,
beside itself from all the screeching,
the huge house, wiggling its arse, is
off into the veld of being.
There they dream silence's dread dream
and hordes of naked factories,
while above the serried ranks of nations
stands the law of labour and creation.

[February 1928]

FOXTROT

Sky-blue leather ankle-boots,
and variegated hosiery,
in the air the hero floats,
wreathed in Hawaian jazz-band steam.
Below, the goblets bray,
below, it's neither night nor day,
below, upon the bandstand seethes
the maistro, like a heathen priest.
He thumps his belly with his fist,
waves his baton in the mist,
and to a carton breast is fixed,
his buoyant cravat's foppish twist.

Hurrah! The hero hovers –
In Lenigrad, Hawaian follies!
Now he folds his arms to make a slab,
now throws one leg across the other,
arching as far back as he can go,
but there's no maiden in front of him;
flying off, one of the cherubim
shakes a leg at those below.

And the ball, a unicorn, resounds,
and women dancing, with much laughter,
display, where sleek limbs intersect,
a siskin on a rosy garter.
The siskin jokes: 'Just take a gander!'
But the women have foregone that zone,
and like a brassy wood out yonder,
pedestalled, the foxtrot drones.

And to these tunes, though it be late,
man has brought into the world
Judas the effeminate,
the loveliest cripple of them all.
Do not disturb him, let him rest,
sleeping the good sleep of a zombie,
with fluffy chick down on his chest,
outgrowth of a wasted body.
And celebrating wine and song,
high above the wretched earth,
our pistol-packing hero, on
a woman, shoots into the air!

[March 1928]

SHAPES OF SLEEP

Checking his flight, beneath the sheets,
a man discovers the shape of sleep.

No moon, but a slender cataract
lures the pans of intellect;
not stars, but canaries of the night,
like ellipses, shining bright.
And in the dark a row of beds,
with slumbering infants end to end;
barely covered,
large white bodies,
sleeping untidily, are nodding.
One of them in a pale-blue gown
hangs across the bed, head-down;
another, stifled by a pillow,
stiffens, dry and scrofulous,
while, a third, plump as an arachnid
casting the tackle of his arms,
passionately snorts and squirms,
fondling imaginary girl-friends.

Meanwhile, behind a sombre hanging,
in the deep ancestral night,
the patriarch sits, his chisel clanging,
and savours wisdom's second sight.
The wardrobe calls to mind King David,
pot-bellied, dozing in his crown;
the couch takes on the part of Eve –
like a wench wrapped in a sheet.
And like the merry little dove
of Noah, a brass lamp in the window,
tripling the darkness, glows,
just as that simple chisel does.

[March 1928]

BAKERY

Dropping into the little quarter,
submissive evening died out soon,
like a light bulb in a glass jar.
The sunset's curious little wounds
kissed the ground and steamed a while;
on the rooftops, cuplike tiles,
like faces met them with a smile
of pure maliciousness, teeth bared.
A cat stuck out its tail and stared.

A bun, twisted into a figure eight,
held up at full tilt on a chain,
began to swing above the shop,
turning itself, on the spot,
into a main character. The baker,
down below, saw dawn like butter
float across the shapes of bread,
nowhere for them to lie low –
everywhere the molten flow,
the pregnant oven snorts and blows,
like Sormov[1] going off its head.

Dough rose, ripping up the trough,
and like a wild beast prowled the shop;
swirling, choking now, it crawled,
its huge snout rubbed against the walls;
the walls creaked, they could not arrest
the cloying dough's triumphant march.
Already the jerked up logs were howling,
but now, passing through mist and rain,
holding a hexagonal lamp,
the leader beat on a frying-pan –
and like idols, bakers swam,
in tiaras, through the mist,
on cymbals playing as they drifted
an unfamiliar can-can.

Like banners, lavishly adorned,
shovels weightily proceeded,

and shiny earthen pots of dough
sailed into the square orifice.
And in this metamorphosing
cave that reddened with the strain,
the infant bread raised up its arms
and a few choice words proclaimed.
The baker blew a fiery call
and trumpeted its fame abroad.

But having produced an heir, the oven,
setting its graceful belly straight,
stood there, bashful as a maid,
a night-rose blooming on its breast.
And in the place of honour, a cat
blessed with a weary paw that snout,
twirled its malodorous little tail,
and then sat on there like a jug.
It sat and sat and smiled its smile,
then vanished. On the clayey floor
a boggy patch was left behind.
And out into the corner flowed the dawn.

[April 1928]

1. Sormov *raion*, in Nizhny Novgorod, a very noisy quarter of the town.

THE LOOP CANAL

Through my window, the Loop Canal
lords it over the whole locale.

Carters entangle horses in
harness, with brassy bits and bobs,
shirted padishahs, filled
with the pomposity of slobs.
Beerhouses have gathered round,
in them weary carters sit,
and through the window, equine faces
peer, pulling on their traces,

and through the window a bank
of equine faces peers point blank.
And beyond this equine court, the crowd
flows on for a quarter of a mile;
with steely fingers sticking out,
in a glowing chorus, blindmen file.
A hawker hurling pants to the sky,
claps his hands, gives a falconish cry;
the hawker, sovereign lord of trousers,
commands the planets in their courses,
the movements of the crowd commands –
it is putty in his hands;
and now, having lost all sense of shame,
powerless to look away,
in helpless rapture, there it stands!

Whistle, hawker, give a shout,
fling those trousers to the sky!
But before the close-packed crowd,
another stream is trickling by;
one man holds a dish, a boot
in it; a silly pooch
another lauds; a third, rubicund and grim,
beats a saucepan, like a drum.
And none can hold out any longer:
the crowd is trapped, the crowd is bonded,
the crowd, like a somnumbalist,
stretches its arms in front of it.

Factories, like castles, lour,
their whistles looping overhead,
and here the mustangs come once more,
a colonnade of splendid legs.
And wagons, wailing plaintively,
spatter trouser-leg and vest,
and by the canal cripples sleep,
pressing empties to their breast.

[June 1928]

STROLLING MUSICIANS

Hefting the pipe onto his back,
like a serpent or a siren,
on foot he flows along with it
towards Gehenna, pining,
wherein's a roar, wherein's a howl
and the glittering flight of money –
that's how the old musician came.

Two others followed, running.
One, hugged a shadowy violin,
wagging it like foliage;
he was a hunchbacked, freelancing, parasitic lout,
his arms like straying tentacles,
his juicy armpits giving out
malodorous, extended drawls.

The second one was fighting fit,
champion of the guitar, a
mighty sacrum in his grip,
with the splendid song, Tamara.[1]
And on it seven iron strings,
by a skilful hand assembled,
and seven shafts, and seven pins –
angularly dangled.

Over roomy streets and squares,
the sun set, and a gang of carters,
with the look of yokels, trotted past
on horses, mountainous and shaggy.
And in the window-circled well,
the snake unwound, a coppery curl,
lifted up a blunt-nosed muzzle,
let out a howl... A toneless eagle
was the first note. It fell; they roared;
after, a second eagle soared;
the eagles turned into cuckoos;
the cuckoos dwindled into dots,
and the dots, with constricted throats,
flew through the windows of each house.

Then the hunchback, with his chin
flattening the violin,
traced a risible grimace
on his abbreviated face,
and the cross-piece with a squeal
sawing at the little strings,
the crippled one began to weep –
tilim-tam-tam-tilim!

The system set out by the book,
imagination led it where
every listener, with a look
about him, wiped away a tear,
when leaning over the window-sills
hung the crowd of doughty fans,
in the music and the din,
arrayed in pants and cardigans.

But the divine of worldly passion
and champion guitarist
lifted the sacrum and its parts
adjusted; then with parted lips
he crooned Tamara's tender song.
All were silent...
The autocratic notes,
muffled like the River Kura,[2]
sumptuous as a daydream,
flew...
And in them, Tamara, without breeches,
on a Caucasian couch reclined,
the stream of her bifurcated back
shone, and youths stood there as well.
And youths stood there,
flapping their arms.
And the wild, p-p-passionate notes
all night r-r-rang out!
Tilim-tam-tam!

The singer was a stern-faced man,
handsome too, he sang and sang,
labouring in the cesspools tall,

straight-backed, muscular and all.
And round him a feline system whirled,
system of buckets, windows, kindling
hung, replicating the dark world
in those narrow courtyard kingdoms.
But what was the yard? A tube,
a tunnel leading to that realm
where Tamara, warrior queen,
slept, and my youth upon the vine
withered, where coins grew numb
in the lamp's uncertain shine,
and flew to the golden serpent's feet
to dance there, tumbling into time!

[August 1928]

1. & 2. References to a popular romance, told by Lermontov.

BATHERS

Monkish man who quits the stove
to climb into a bath or basin,
come and bathe now in the river,
cast aside all things distasteful!

Who hides his rooster with his hand
falls in with a resounding shock,
swims with the company, in the van –
from his groin comes only smoke!

All who first take off their clothes
and also various bits of armour,
may start like ignoramuses,
but excellent progress follows after.

Liquid, like a tender goose,
nibbles parts of youthful bodies,
with a dark-blue hand it soothes
those who are all hot and sticky.

If a person has no desire
to remain a long time soaking,
he can towel himself dry
with a cloth of air-and-ochre.

If a person's subject to
temptation, or is overcome
by passion, he can cool
his ardour there, with both eyes shut.

If a person cannot love,
but is by longing often gnawed,
he can give himself a shove
and float along there with a board.

O, river, O betrothed, O nanny,
you grant everyone asylum,
you're no simple wench or female,
but a saint, as in an icon!

No simple wench or female you,
you're the holy Saint Praskovya,[1]
where there's sand and milky spurge.
greet us bathers with a surge!

[September 1928]

1. The patron saint of women's work.

IMMATURITY

The infant makes a bowl of porridge,
pale-blue seeds of semolina;
a particle, like a toy brick,
shoots from feathery, twofold fingers.
Grain by grain the bowl is filled,
and, suspended, swings there now,
like bells in a belfry tolled,
renowned for their quadrate power.

The infant crawls through bristling thickets,
from the nut-trees plucks some leaves,
and with fluttering fingers picks at
the underneath-him tops of trees.
And girls, gathered in that place,
float towards him on a cloud;
one removes a little cross,
slowly drifting to the ground.
The bowl is swirling underfoot,
the fiery substance is alive,
and she lies there in the nude,
her lacey things cast in the fire.
Softly the infant answers her:
'I'm a child, still tottery,
in your port how can I berth,
when love has not yet blinded me?
Since your beauty makes me blush,
cover your nakedness, and please –
see how my bonfire burns! –
spare me your profanities!'
And calmly picking up the stirrer,
sagaciously he stirred the bowl.
Thus, did he a practical
in science give the troubled soul.

[September 1928]

THE PEOPLE'S HOUSE[1]

1.

All the world is papered over,
love's little grotto this,
windows hardly more than fissures,
curtains with a rose-motif.
Favourite photographs of friends
are pinned up fan-like by the table.
'O, no more nights that have no end...'
As loud as it is able,
the copper instrument intones,

the wooden belly sobs and moans,
hurry, hurry, honeyed slut –
girls sit here on their own –
arms hang vertically down,
skin is peeling in the sun,
noses scale, and second-hand
faces flatten. Girls sit here,
braiding into bast mats their hair,
fluffing up their plump beds: 'We're
so very happy, sit around
in circles waiting to be found.
She will come, the fair enchantress,
and suitors, too, will come on wheels –
they'll doff their caftans, then pronounce
heartfelt sentiments, and we'll
keep fondling their manly hands,
and laughing, with that special look,
and then we'll pull our stockings up –
See, how long our legs, how classic! –
a wee bit higher than the knee!'
And so these innocent young lasses,
chattered together festally,
playing games with destiny...

But what care they for fate as such,
when there is fire in the blood,
when sentiments, like foamy puffs,
sensationlike, drift by above?
In a tram, the folks are moving,
crossing Kronversky in the window,
and like oil-lamps faces glow,
dresses bloom with bright red tulips,
sweaty, trying to be lovely –
they bob around like chintzy plums,
and their arms forever stretching,
stretching ever further out –
and here it is, upside down,
the People's House.

2.

The People's House, hencoop of pleasure,
granary of beguiling life,
trough of passion and of leisure,
sweltering bustle of the hive!
Here are spiked red-army helmets,
and with them ladies easy-going,
drifting in a dreamy stream,
oblivious of the city's din;
here pleasure crooks a finger,
offers each one wholesome fun,
here every lad can drown his cares,
tendering his lady nuts,
or passing out over the beer.
Here is the rollercoaster range
and lovely girls, like goddesses,
huddling in the speeding cars;
the cars roll forward with élan,
the gentle things, in floods of tears,
collapse about their cavaliers...

Here's a wench, her little doggy
immaculate on a lasso.
She herself is soaked right through,
her bosom riding to the fore.
And that excellent, upright pooch,
brimming with the sap of spring,
rustles awkwardly along
on stubby mushroom legs.

An orange-vendor, splendid fellow,
approaches this distinguished wench;
he holds a multi-coloured vessel,
in which the fruits precisely rest.
Resilient and corrugated,
they are like circles, compass-drawn,
solar miniatures, they swish
freely about the tin-plate dish
and burble: pick me, pick me, miss!

And munching fruit, the girl bestowed
a rouble on the passing stranger,
addressed him with a plain hullo,
but it's another that she favours.
Her eyes searched for this gallant,
when a swing whistled out in front.

A sweet thing, seated on the swing,
rubbed her dainty feet together –
rustling, she flew through the air,
twirled a little foot out there,
and tipped a hand invitingly.

Another, having caught sight of his face,
refracted in a humpbacked mirror,
stood like a lackey in disgrace,
tried laughter, but could not be led.
Wishing to know what was the cause,
he became an infant, as it were,
backing from it, on all fours,
a close-on forty quadruped.

Scarcely had the uproar ceased,
than the rush was under way again.
People were all puffed up with breath,
girls were huddling together.
Already walking was not easy,
descending streamwards, they dispersed,
scattering here and there in pairs,
sinking onto tender knees.

           3.
But others seem to have given up
before this holiday intoxication –
the barn of pleasure's not enough,
they often came here in their youth.
And now, mumbling to a bottle,
bidding fiery youth farewell,
they scrape their teeth across the glass,
with their lips they vacuum it,
and in The Bavaria tell tales

of rumbustious merry-makings.
The bottle's like a mother to them,
a soul-mate, sluttish and sweet-tongued,
kisses more honeyed than a wench's,
and more cooling than the Nevka...

They gaze out of the window.
In the window morning glows.
A lamp, pale as a tapeworm, droops
in the shrubbery, like a dart.
Now paradise is a swaying tram,
where every boychik cracks a smile,
while on the other hand, each girl
shuts her eyes and parts her lips,
and on the soft curve of her belly,
lets a warm arm flop.

The tram, just barely, doesn't stop...

[1927–1928]

1. The People's House, a theatre-club, built before the Revolution, with an amusement
park attached. The 1965 'Sovietsky Pisatel' edition of Zabolotsky's poems contains
the following note: 'A curious commentary for this poem can be found in
Leningradskaya Pravda (5 June 1926): "In the grounds of the People's House, one
of the most capacious amusement parks in Leningrad... a petty provincial life goes
on... You can hardly get about for all the drunks... Concert turns at hourly intervals,
switchbacks and distorting mirrors – that's all the People's House has to offer its
public." This notice provoked some lively responses in subsequent issues.'

Long Poems

Agriculture Triumphant

Not so good but good to look at,
who's this man that's peering at us
through his specs? Why, it's a kulak
slow of foot and short of purpose.
Barns in glittering incandescence
loom up whitely in the distance,
rye is peeping through the window,
in the yard, with arms akimbo,
sits a horse, while Nature's sprawling
in quite maddening disorder.
Here a tree reels, nearly falling,
while a wispy river's scrawled there.
A few peasant huts are standing
by the loony little brook,
and an oblong bear is ambling,
late of evening, to his nook,
while a crane, a monstrous creature,
wags his head in laboured, freakish
flight, and fills the silent sky
with his whooping battle cry...
His beak unfurls a slogan: 'Listen!'
cries the scroll: 'The Three Field System's
Unproductive.' The peasant stared
and pensively stroked the end of his beard...

Translator's note: While visiting Nikita Zabolotsky in Moscow, I happened to
catch a radio adaptation of this poem. The original is divided into episodes,
as here, but individual speaking-parts are not assigned throughout. I have
taken the liberty of so assigning them, as in the radio adaptation and as in the
other poems in this section.

ONE
[A discussion about the soul]

Narrator
Night has taken to the air,
in the school the students doze,
winking lanterns, here and there,
hanging from the peasants' homes.
The peasant men have gathered round;
they have come here to discuss
where a man's soul's to be found?
Maybe all that's left of us
after death's a speck of dust,
or perhaps only stinking gasses?
On pinkish poles, the starling-houses
float above them, like a cloud.
The lowering peasants, amply shod
in the felt boots of their lot,
sit, with whiskers all puffed out –
their headgear, too, is sticking up,
like top heavy dunoon caps.
Idly snapping canine brutes
lounge between their masters' boots.
A peasant, with a face like thunder,
holds a milk jug on his knee:

Peasant
Nature's certainly no mother,
she makes an old man out of me!
When I'm striding, like a giant,
across my fields, behind the plough,
I stare and stare, because in front
it's always there, that ghostly crowd.

Elderly peasant
True! Some kind of animal spirit
lives among us, disembodied.
For let me tell you, brothers,
it's a fearful mess, is nature,
and the beasts that share our quarters
aren't at all what they once were...
Who's this...

Soldier

Don't tell whoppers, dad!
Only a ninny would be glad
to hear you carrying on like that!
We've seen a lot of fighting,
me and my horse, been through the wars,
but I've never heard such whining,
or such scary tales as yours.
I'm telling you, friends, that nature
doesn't understand a thing...
You'd better not rely on it!

Herdsman

Who can tell?
All my life, I've herded cows.
Nature as a whole's a home –
look, I'm getting angry now!
You peasants, living in the world,
prize your wretched little huts.
Me, I've always much preferred
nature's doghouse, clean and snug.
Cows make a lot more sense to me
than your lot! Why, from birth
you've been weak and feeble and
as ignorant as sin!

Second Peasant

It's you who're ignorant! Excuse
me breaking in, but otherwise
me and you will come to blows.
Tell me, cross your heart and hope to die,
do the souls of dead men rise?

Narrator

A biddy's busy with her knitting.
A cowshed angles sharply out,
a tree lounges like a lout.
Through the log walls of the hut,
ovens shine, armour-plate,
and cubicly refract the light,
with the chimney square's upright.

The mysterious cradle poles
creak and sigh like hollow bones,
in them unsmiling infants doze,
flee-bitten, from head to toe.
A peasant, bent over a bucket,
washes fiercely by the stove.
Another mends his horse's bridle.
A third is striking sparks from stone...

Woman
Peasant, come to bed... All right?

Narrator
A woman's crying,
And like a little mother, night
rocks the village, sighing.

Herdsman
Yonder, in the cemetery,
their soul is floating, oh so lovely,
I can't find words to tell about it!
A rooster, sitting on a birch,
has crowed a dozen times today.
Frost-bite's got its feet, its perch
is hard to grip, it flies away.
But with a shiny, shiny hand,
the soul, far off, is waving, see!
Its body's like a thunder-cloud,
its dress to me seems like a stream.
Its eyes, still tender, look at us,
they look at us, and yet its body
is eaten up by worms and sodden,
in its dark and narrow house...

Soul
People, people, listen to me!
I'm the same as all of you.
But my breasts have shrivelled,
and grass roots bind my hair.
Take me as your sweetheart, take me,
to lie alone here is so hard!

Speak to me a little, people,
just speak to me, that's all I ask!

Old Peasant
It's very sad, there's no denying!
Our pet, our little darling, flying.
I ran into her one night,
as I was sucking on my pipe.
Straight towards me from the grave,
in a column, on she came,
and waved at me with her hand
to join her in that other land!
But no sooner had I hopped into
that yard, than up she flew,
perched a moment, and was gone!

Soldier
I can see what's going on!
Here, superstition's all the rage,
But, old fellow, you'd best take
back what you've just said. Listen,
There's a simple explanation.
I've been through the wars, like I said,
bullets whistling overhead.
But now I've something else to say
concerning our topic here to day.
Particles of phosphorus flit,
evaporating from the pit,
and carried onward by the air,
this little phosphorescent column
floats all over, except where
it happens to bump into something solid.
And that's about all there is to it!

Narrator
The peasants fall silent now,
long of jaw, dark of brow.
On rosy poles, the starling-houses
float above them all, like cloudlets.
The lantern lights are burning low,
in school the students doze.

Calmly a woman teacher stares
far into the greying fields,
where night, like a prankster, drowns its cares,
and Aquarius faintly gleams.
The dim shapes of the creatures cluster,
their bodies filling up the barn.
They're having a free-for-all discussion,
nature's soul within their grasp.

TWO
[Sufferings of the animals]

Narrator
The bodies of the creatures,
seated dimly in the barn,
they are all conversing freely,
nature's soul within their grasp.
Night, a prankster on the eaves,
scares the praying mantises,
and Aquarius revolves,
spilling a slick stream of tin
over the white window-sill.
The creatures, crowding there,
stretch their composite bulk and sit
darkly, with a vacant air.

Bull
Myself, I'm hard for me to mark!
Consciousness has left its mark,
but I am old and weary now.
What am I to make of all my doubts?
How set the troubled mind at ease?
Thank god, the day has passed without
mishap ... Or so it seems!
But here not everything's so plain,
sorrow's grabbed me by the throat.
As you can see, I'll soon be laid
in our bovine burial moat.
Funereal groaning,
doleful wailing!

No individual grave, no railing.
A dead cow's simply thrown
into a pit among the bones
of lambs, while a dog snaps at a hawk
and gnaws a wretched creature's corpse.
The hoof of some poor beast decays,
making fodder for a plant,
and a worm, corruption's mate,
straddles a skull that lies apart.
Shreds of eyeball matter, skin,
bone and gristle everywhere.
Only the dew drops, spattered there,
still quake and quiver, glittering!

    Horse
The enlightened are not scared
by the pale horseshoe of death.
Mortals have a greater need
for life's grievous truth.
Drawn out like a plug of aspic,
in the narrow, sloping home
of its oblong skull, my active
brain's no lie-abed, no drone!
You are wrong, men, if you think
me incapable of thought,
when you beat me with a stick,
fix a harness round my throat.
A peasant grips me between his thighs,
hits me savagely with his knout,
and when I gallop, what a sight,
gulping air with sunken mouth!
All around me nature's dying.
In its wretchedness, the world
falters, flowers weep, expiring,
by my flying hooves annulled.
Of his injuries taking stock,
another shuts his eyes, lies down,
but the peasant on my back,
like a demon,
waves his arms and legs about.
In my stall, I stand and stew,

forlorn. The pallid glow
of consciousness is shining through
a window opened long ago.
And now, my sore legs giving way,
I listen... The heavens howl,
a beast shudders, it's his fate
to keep the system going round.
Open your eyes, I beseech you,
must every human be our leader?

Narrator
A crude awareness grips them all,
as if they had been turned to stone.
The creatures, taken as a whole,
are like corpses, skin and bone.
Filled with kerosene, the lamp
quakes in tortured incandescence,
flickering and so ancient that
it verges upon non-existence.
Like suffering's sullen offspring,
memories gather, jostling
in the brains of stubborn animals.
It seems, the binary world's been torn,
and beyond the raw edge of that fabric
a pale expanse of blue is born!

Bull
I can see a dreary graveyard.
In a damp pit, half devoured,
who is this, miserable, scabby,
fast asleep and all forgotten,
the wretched graveyard's denizen,
a dingy wreath on top of him?
Throwing up their pallid arms,
nights around him pine and gutter,
funereally draped in webs.
About the sleeper, flowers mutter,
while round him, unseen by men,
stout as oak-trees, only straight,
those intelligent witnesses of his life tower,
The Tables of Fate.[1]

And all read with harmonious eyes
the strange corpse's conjecturings,
and the animal world is reconciled
in foolish splendour with the heavens.
And many centuries shall pass,
our sickly progeny shall pale,
but even they'll find peace at last
on the shores of such a grave.
So a man, the century left behind,
in Novgorodian silt now cast,[2]
the lovely image of his kind,
impressed on nature's soul at last!

> *Narrator*
> Incredulous, they fall into a trance,
> the horse sticks out his lip and dreams,
> and nights, as at the outset, prance.
> From roof to stack the pranksters leap,
> then fall. A sudden light explodes,
> the orb is rising now, majestic,
> while birds, above the oaks, carol,
> witnesses of these dialectics.

1. Refers to a long poem, *The Tables of Fate*, by the Futurist poet Velemir Khlebnikov.
2. Lit. 'buried in the Novgorodian mud', referring to Khlebnikov's grave.

THREE
[The outcast]

> *Narrator*
> Birds, above the oaks, carol,
> witnesses of these dialectics,
> and Aquarius glows, upon the soil
> shedding his primary luminescence,
> while over the village, standing high,
> still changeful, still as dark,
> encircled by its ancient shine,
> rises the Russian moon at last...

The cottage stands there, like a fort,
snug inside the blighted world,

showing its owner how absurd
are kolkhoz, freedom and hard work.
The kulak, blind as a feudal lord,
says:

> *Voice of Kulak*
>   This land is mine, by God!
> This is my new cattle-shed.
> This is my house, this is my bed.

> *Narrator*
He turns and tosses through the night,
as growling dogs patrol outside.

Coins with the heads of kings on them
locking away in heavy coffers,
he is an outcast among men,
and terror is his constant
companion, while in their icon-cases
gods glower, thinking hard.
Feeble bipeds, shaggy faces,
ⲓ ⲓⲓⲱ ⲓⲓ ⲓⲦ, Ⲓⲓ ⲁⲓ ⲓⲓⲓⲓⲓ, Ⲓⲓⲁⲓⲓ ₋ⲉⲦⲓⲓⲓ ⲓ Ⲓ ⲁⲓⲦ,
with large, uncommon beards,
from behind the glass they stare
at where the man, with folded arms,
is breaking into slow salaams.

The kulak gives himself to prayer,
dogs howl, the fates keep watch,
and time takes clumsily to the air,
following the bank downstream.
Nature gives grudgingly of sap,
plants fill to the brim with silence,
sluggishly the grasses sprout,
stunted, sickly, feeble, eyeless.
In need of powerful salts, the earth
beseeches him: 'Kulak, how long?'
But notwithstanding all its threats,
the kulak decimates his crops.
He ruins, time and time again,
those tokens of tomorrow, and
surrendering to fatigue, the grain,
now losing heart, can barely stand.

The kulak, the farm labourers' lord,
sits there, by his wealth extolled,
and his egocentric world
rises higher than many a cloud.
And night bestirs its straggly limbs,
scurrying witchlike over roofs,
now looses on the fields the wind,
now hides away and holds its breath,
now tears a shutter from its haven,
crying:

Voice of Night
   Rise, accursed raven!
Above us roars the hurricane.
Seize it, grasp the hand it offers,
unravel the barbed entanglement,
or else, along with your fat coffers,
you'll die, all movement at an end!

Through battle, thunder and through work,
I see the mighty currents surge,
I see the Dnieper, stone-encased,
submerged in flames, the Caucasus.
An iron horse is bringing grain,
a cast-iron ox is hauling kvass.
The plough and harrow lift and draw,
turn and break the hoary soil.
From now on, ancient raven, you're
accountable to it for all!

Narrator
The kulak, sitting on a bench,
rakes his sturdy flank and howls.
And a dog senses trouble up ahead –
stockaded in by legs, it yowls.
And then we hear the soldier's gong,
and creaking doors, and in a while
a solitary figure's gone
like a thief into the night.
Outcast of the world and skinflint,
he listens to the small bells tinkling.

Mentally he salutes his hut,
like a drunk swaying in his cart.
And night, the day's progenitor,
with determination now,
witchlike, from the roof swoops down,
upending that impenitent!

FOUR
[The battle with the ancestors]

Narrator
Night resounds in tub and jar,
in hollow pine, in the tempest's pipes,
night, in an idol's mask,
flashes like lapis lazuli,
night like a petty tyrant blusters,
chaos all about,
a wolf, struck by a stub of plaster,
whirls by weeping, rubs his snout.
A boar, a fly, a motley band
of birds, torn from the pine trees, cry:
'It's more than flesh and blood can stand!
The wind is just too much tonight!'
And to cap it all, lugubriously
howling, a bear trots past; tears pour
down his sore face, ruefully
covered by outspread jumbo paws:
'Night, just you go to hell!
Leave us alone, Beelzebub!'
And Night replies: 'I will! I will!'
The wind is blowing, there's the rub.
Aye, the accursed wind, I'm saying,
like gun-powder exploding, spraying...
Well, so much for your Russian North,
where the trees lack all support!

Soldier
I hear the fury of the wind,
and I hear the tempest's howl,
but I am used to it, my mind

knows there's no devil here, no ghoul,
there's no bogey-man, no mermaid,
no wood-goblin, horrid gnome,
just the battling sounds the trees make.
There'll be calm after the storm.

Ancestors
No telling, really, though it's easy
to see why you would think so.
Patchy clouds drift by above us,
and a huge pit yawns below.
Only you, a child of reason,
nurturing unhealthy thoughts from birth,
think it just some kind of teasing,
as winds collide above the earth.

Soldier
Dread ancestors, stop it!
You abominable moles,
keep your mouths buttoned up,
quit fiddling with the soil!
You dare to threaten me
with some incomprehensible punishment!
Before you take your leave,
explain: Just what do you want?

Ancestors
We *are* the ancestors, yours too.
For those who have so much to do,
we cleave the century in two,
and what we now propose is to
set limits on your fantasies.
We prefer those average
types who simply propagate,
those who dance and those who sing,
those who don't intimidate,
those who don't *make* anything.

Soldier
How's that! Your stupidity
is insufferable! Worse than death!

That truth of yours
has turned into pigheadedness.
At night, lying on my bed,
I see a naked woman. She's
sitting there, without a dress,
rising to her apogee
and reeking of milk ... Ancestors, *dear*,
what's so special about this?
By the hammer I declare
clothing's greatly to be wished!

    Ancestors
Whatever you are, she's no fool,
the woman's simply nature's vessel.
Her figure's noble as a rule,
two infants tugging at her nipples.
One she cuddles with her palm
beneath his rear-end, while his peer
is lying curled up on her bosom,
stinking up the atmosphere.

    Soldier
Even so, I still can't see
why she should appeal to me!

    Ancestors
We'll explain. A woman's belly
is cast in a complicated mould.
It supplies the spirit's dwelling
for all of nine months in a row.
The infant, in a Buddha pose,
soon receives a human set,
its little headpiece grows and grows,
so that thought might effervesce,
and so the limbs should keep evolving,
the umbilical cable,
like a long-drawn out proboscis,
is firmly plugged into the navel.

    Soldier
Ancestors, I know all that,

yet we'd do well to cogitate:
Wouldn't we be going back,
if all we did was propagate?

Ancestors
Scum, riff-raff, dregs piled high,
abortion of some cross-eyed jade.
Your reasoning is out of mind,
it's been *differently* made!
Winds, bash down his sturdy hammer,
pines, smash through the rascal's liver,
so he never more shall jabber,
split in two right down the middle!

Soldier
Hold your tongue! Be off! If not,
I'll shoot you down right on the spot!
The dead should stay where they've been laid,
and so... look lively! To the grave!
Let priests moan over you and let
the devils howl and cry,
you ancestors have no effect
on me. I'll live until I die!

Narrator
At this time, an oak, appalled,
splits in two. A wolf, put out,
on three legs rushes past, a paw
lifted to protect his snout.
A boar, a fly, a whole assembly
of ants, also a good-sized otter,
whirl by, helter skelter,
and the trees claw at them, Gotcha!
Only the soldier, well protected
by his helmet, greatcoat buttoned,
rises, like the Beelzebub of
fields that have been left untended.
And a midnight bird, a haunter
of these pleasant, grassy parts,
having broken off a branch.
brings the man a drop of water.

FIVE
[The birth of science]

Narrator
As the bird at midnight flies
grandly over rippling grass,
the peasants' faces come alive,
feeling the sudden stormy blast.
Above the world of bitter sorrows
resounds a shepherd's clarinet,
a rooster crows, and morning follows,
and the bovine tribute swells.
And over the oak grove brightly lifts
that luminary, filled with gifts.

Praise the world, and peace on earth!
Master and monied man, be damned!
The red atom of rebirth
is borne off by morning in its palm.
The red atom of rebirth,
that torch of life incarnadine,
whose movements here on earth
flood the land with cinnabar.
People and their cattle rise,
horses, oxen rise up too,
and look, the soldier now arrives,
clad in scarlet, head to toe!
In the mighty herd, who's he –
the devil's own or maybe god's?
See, his star, equipped with wings,
gleams like a rhinoceros!

Soldier
Cattle, listen to my dream.
In my sheepskin, I was sleeping,
and the horizon parted to reveal
a lofty Institute of Creatures.
There, the air was fresh and sweet,
and in the centre of that place
stood a fine cow, full of grace,
its consciousness still incomplete.

Goddess of Milk, Goddess of Cheese,
brushing the ceiling with her head,
bashfully she raised her frieze
and thrust her dugs into a keg.
Ten streams descended with a crash,
pounding the hammered-metal vat,
and the can, ready for dispatch,
blared like a military band.
And that ecstatic cow stood tight,
her arms folded across her chest,
game for anything that might
ameliorate her consciousness.

    Cows
What you say is strange, we find,
knowing, as we do, the human mind!
But, anyhow, what happened after that?
How did the other creatures act?

    Soldier
After that I saw a torch
in the brainy bullock's halls,
and a curia of cows
was debating its affairs.
Cackling at them, a silly ass
ran all over, belching trash.
In its thick head, reason's plant
shone feebly, not unlike the grass.
The ass went hiking through the hills,
chewing potatoes of cast-iron,
while a temple of industry below
turned out pills of oxygen.
Chemistry's good friend, the horse
slurped hundred-molecule soup with grace,
others, in the air, kept watch
for visitors from outer space.
Draped in tapes and formulae,
a cow baked an elemental pie,
while before them, in a cup,
big-eared chemical oats sprang up.

Horse
What an admirable place –
nothing but fun and games, and science!
Listening to the soldier's tales,
it feels like I've had my fill of wines!
At first, my mind was quite confused –
I was in a fine old sweat!
Can it be what you say is true,
young soldier? Is the plough now dead?
Besides our sinews, can it be that
intellect's now required and so forth?
Listen – me, I'm an old hand,
and medals are all I've got to show for it.
I've struggled with the plough for ages,
and suddenly chemistry – teehee! – the rage is!

Soldier
Silence, fleabag, crowbait!
Can't you see I've more to say?
Your witty observations don't
amount to a heap of hay.
My mind's no different from yours,
a pan with sawdust, nothing more,
but with such a sight before your eyes,
do your best, horseflesh, to be wise!
So...
   Over the Equine Institute,
gracefully the moon then rose,
pots got a scientific break,
and the axle's hour drew close.
The ass, a comrade leading him,
arrives now, hungry, with a limp.
And so they feed him, like a child,
to stimulate his plantlike mind.
Here the butterfly becomes a worker,
the grass-snake learns a little science –
how to spin yarn, how to make mica,
how to run up gloves and pants.
A wolf, with an iron microscope,
serenades the evening star,
while a horse talks in lengthy tropes

with dill, raddish and cauliflower.
And graceful choirs of human beings,
leaving the fields of heaven, drop
onto the hayricks of the world
to partake of the godly food of swans!

>   *Horse*
Are you done?

>   *Soldier*
>   Done.
>   *Horse*
>   Bravo! Bravo!
My dear, I thought you'd never end!
How sweet your poison is and, oh,
I'm burning up from what you said!
Here we go naked and barefoot,
weighed down by ploughs and stung by wasps,
our minds like squalid rows of huts,
our tails trail in the dust, like rods.
At the hour of the midnight watch,
in the smoke of autumn evenings,
soldier, have you heard the wheezings
of your poor, tormented ox?
No help for us, we've got no rights,
the plough calls and the ranks of graves.
For those who no longer make the grade,
death is the only State in sight!

>   *Soldier*
What are you babbling on about!
Shame on you! What's up, horse!
Just look who's crawling round
the hill, to take your place.
Metal, two-storeys high it stands,
with cast-iron snout and spitting fire,
master of combat, hand-to-hand,
with nature…it's coming here.
Take heart, you cows of intellect,
take heart, you bullocks and you horses,
henceforth, sanitary quarters,

for all of you we shall erect.
Overthrowing plough and harrow,
we'll raze the old world to the ground,
and for the first time, in a mighty choir,
the letter 'A' we shall pronounce!

> *Narrator*

And so the distant forests growl,
remotely echoing that 'A',
and a tractor rumbles out –
with its snout it cleaves the age.
And crowds of helpless animals,
sprawling in the dust and dirt,
gaze with shining eyes primeval
upon the new face of the earth.

SIX
[The infant world]

> *Narrator*

As the gathering of beasts
sings the victory of the earth,
peasants from fertile granaries
bring all their possessions forth.
Some of them, huge men with beards,
arrive with wooden ploughs and spades,
others drag into the light
millenial hoes – a hoary sight!
Like a pile of skulls, the mound
rises of instruments of torture,
and the grim tractor driver counts
a hundred years of wasted labour.

> *Tractor Driver*

People, it is very odd!
Waste like this you can't digest.
The he-goat of antiquity trots,
sharp stones spattering his breast.
Peasant, bonded to the hoe,
bonded to the lanky shovel,

you were a slave, but even so
you never were the rich man's plaything.
You destroyed the house of bondage,
now you're building a kolkhoz,
a tractor of the second bronze age
hauls your unprecedented crops.
Long-shanked and desiccated,
the plough is superannuated!
New Age, it's time that it began!
Greetings to you, horse and man!

Plough
Enough of prophesying doom!
Little man, don't play the fool!
I'm the plough, the harvest queen,
the tractor shall not have my bones.
My torso's firmly knit between
and up the sides with solid oak.
On my belly, merrily,
fleas guffaw, and leaping high,
the god of private property
prances, jabbing at the sky.
Private property's young lad
on my belly jumps and stamps,
like an orb the earthly globe
quickens underneath his hand.
Surrender to his power, crawl,
inside you sounds his bugle-call!

Tractor Driver
Goddess,
your time has long since passed,
nor did your sister titans last.
We are constructing a new world,
a brand new sun and brand new grass.
We take our leave of you, as with
a hero, or a faithful hound...
Give the poor old plough a hand!

Narrator
Breaking away from algebra,

little boys race by in packs,
panicking, a female swarm,
with chubby babes, falls on all fours.
Oven smoke flies in the air,
overhead a long black slur.
The rooster sings his tipsy lay,
above the huts the light of day.
Sealed tight with a log of dung,
the church's long cocoon is shaken,
light flails the dust of sleep, which from
the windows streams over dour faces.
From the laths there hangs a swarm
of bats, suspended heads down, twitching,
as if a flock of defunct witches
had sought sanctuary in this Third Rome.
And then a raspy toxin sounds.
On sturdy shoulders born aloft,
floats the plough, an ancient reptile,
its straight shafts rounded like a loaf,
approaching now. It speaks
the last words it will ever utter –
the half-open grave is
its implacable instructor.
And before that silent crowd,
the new world, born in toil and pain,
nodding its fledgling infant's head,
recites the ABC again.

SEVEN
[Agriculture Triumphant]

   Narrator
Morning comes, the fog's begun
to lift, trundling off the field.
Like blind men breaking out of line,
poplars scatter through the weald.
Choirs of sowing-machines, on track,
weighing out kilograms of seed,
move in a row. The ploughman beams,
from exposure to the sun burnt black.

Various activities proceeding,
people sit around in groups,
some busy with their mending,
others drawing on their pipes.
An old man, squatting in a gully,
imparts philosophy to his dog.
Another, likewise king and god
of agricultural implements,
fingers a cow's resilient dugs
and her shins, like fine hard rods.
Patiently he then expounds
his notion of precision threshers,
and explains it to the cows,
with relish laying out his sketches.

Wooden villages are gathered
along the hilltop, gazing down.
In his shed, an ass lauds nature,
now that his mind is fully grown.
The lazy separator whirls,
and there are lots of laughing girls.
Others who, at break of day,
have cast their nets, are gutting perch.
The family soup is simmering,
flame and cooking pot converse,
and man, chewing, marvels at
what he himself has brought to birth.

The soldier, too, is sitting here.
His mind is teeming with ideas.

Soldier
Renowned Agriculture!
Machines, already half in place!
Ploughmen, no more idle banter,
there'll be victuals, there'll be hay.
Arm yourself with the precise
science of binders, the sectioning of udders!
You'll be sorry otherwise,
your minds uncouth, untutored sluggards.
The Theory of Labour Formation
has taught our chapped hands what to do.

Good sciences, all praise to you,
and, kolkhoz–cities, salutations!

    Narrator
And now a cheerful hum
of approval spreads across,
and the soldier lifts his mug,
and thirstily chugs down the kvass.
Chief executive of crop–rotation
and nature's ardent farrier,
he beats his military staves
into sickles then and there.
And chariots of hardy rye,
weighing as much as houses, rock,
trundling along the boundary line,
hauled by a tractor made of bronze.

But on the hill above the river,
cemetery worms devour,
for the very first time ever,
the wooden body of the plough.
So, the queen of earth is dead,
that peddlar so beloved of crones,
and rising high above her head,
the burdock of oblivion!
And the mournful burdock heaves,
slaps its leaf against the stone,
and over the ramshackle grave,
a sad *te deum* it intones.

The peasants having eaten well,
are now perusing newspapers.
A handsome peasant shaves his beard,
another's practising his letters.
On pipes of clay the infants toot,
smearing dirt fore and aft,
and an evening of forget–me–not
floats through the air and laughs.

[1929–1930]

The Mad Wolf

Hör! Es splittern die Saülen ewig grüner Paläste.
[Goethe: *Faust* Part 1, Walpurgisnacht]

I. CONVERSATION WITH THE BEAR

Bear
The vaults of the evergreen house
have not yet come tumbling down.

We've not been put in enclosures
to gobble up peoples' leftovers.

Under the free-born oak
we enjoy the little we know.

We sing the praises of the sun,
drink plain water and have fun.

Wolf, what is your occupation?

Wolf
Flaying dogs alive,
I watch the stars stream by.
If you happen to come across me lying on my back
with my paws sticking in the air,
it means that the beam of my vision
is directed straight up at the heavens.
After that, I compose songs, explaining
why our necks as yet aren't vertical.
A wizard once said it was surgical –
that the neck he could certainly straighten.
Now tell me: What's *your* occupation.

Bear
One moment! Actually, I chanced upon
a figure lying in the woods.
It lifted two slender feet,
and gazed out towards the east.
Rising straight into the air,
in its bristling coat of fur,
it floated like a fish up where
the sky was just a reddish blur.
Tell me, wolf, how come that beasts
have this urge to gaze upwards?
Isn't it best to follow nature,
looking down, around, or back,
to creep into people's gardens
and keep clear of the beaten track?
Just think, in our modest dens,
where there's neither door nor window,
like gods of old, we shall reign
over domestic and other creatures.
And sometimes we can fool around,
catching birdies on the wing.
Ignoring rifles and revolvers,
we enjoy biting the heads off robins
and throwing then down to our young,
to suck on and have fun...
But, wolf, this was not what you intended,
your horizontal neck upended.

Wolf
Well said, bear! Well said!
I wholeheartedly approve,
myself having bitten off many a head,
when I was splendid in my youth.
But all this belongs to earlier times!
Since then, my horizontal spine
has turned to iron, or call it granite,
and our slim muzzles simply cannot
gaze upward at the source of light.
Meanwhile, a bright star shines above,
Venus; it has a magic grip
with which to grasp the soul and tug

and convulsively to seal the lips.
I ask what is the universe's
size, and are there wolves up there.
But I'm a prisoner, and still worse is
that offal is my usual fare!

Bear
I feel the urge to laugh, and yet
don't wish to hurt his feelings.
This wolf's prepared to dislocate
his neck for just a glimpse of Venus!

Wolf
I shall order a device
for the dislocation of the neck.
I'll lay my head upon it and
struggle hard to turn the wheels.
With this vertical neck, I wager
I will soon be out of favour.
I know I'll be a running joke
with all my friends and womenfolk.
But if the truth I am to learn,
tell me, valiant bear, how can
I not offend my friends, nor turn
from the tenderness of women?
Of lupine life the grand reformer,
though nothing to write home about,
I'll live on like an emperor –
my bit of science gives me that clout!
So as to cover certain places,
I'll make myself a canvas blazer,
I'll illuminate my lare,
install a bed and a pisspot too,
and I'll attempt, within a year,
to make my sciences bear fruit.

Bear
The vaults of the evergreen house
have not yet come tumbling down.
And we still have such ones in our midst
as this demented wolf!

My tender youth has passed,
and sad old age has come at last.
I no longer understand anything,
only the little leaves murmuring above...
So, maybe I'm conservative...
Your ideas I can do without, I'm sorry!
I don't want to learn how to to read and write,
or how to use a lavatory.
I'm a bear. To steal is fun.
I'm the Assurbanipal of cows!
No one's ever shoved a gun
in my introspective snout.
I want to bite! I want to guzzle!
Out of my way! I'm coming through!
You've lost me. It's a puzzle,
what your crazy head's up to.
But I can see it's no use talking.

Wolf
So, bear and I have fallen out.
I may regret it, but god knows,
the bear has kept me on my toes.

2. A MONOLOGUE IN THE FOREST

Up above, the sun and moon
are shining on the wolf's stone home.
The wolf communes with the cuckoo
and to each tree he gives a name.
About his frame, a cotton vest,
breeches flapping round his feet,
like a monk-scribe in his cell,
he sits and covers countless sheets.
Round him, the hills of clay
expose just halves of themselves to the sky,
their other halves in shadow lie,
and so day follows day.

Wolf
[throwing down his pen]
I hope that with this song

I'll have jogged the universe a little,
so I can peek into the future.
I don't know what is going on,
but all the same I like composing songs.
You make a squiggle in a little book,
and suddenly it's singing like an angel!

For ten years,
I've been living in a hut.
I read books, sing songs,
and frequently commune with nature.
My mind has raised itself, my neck is healed.
But the days hurry by. Already I am turning grey,
my backbone creaks from time to time.
Take heart, old fellow, one last effort,
and like a birdy you will fly!

I have discovered a multitude of laws.
For instance, if you put a plant inside a jar
and blow upon it through a metal tube,
the plant fills with breath,
a head appears, and little arms and legs,
and the leaves shrivel up for good.
By sheer force of will,
from a plant I raised a little dog –
now it is crooning like a mother.
And from a birch tree
I had planned to raise a camel,
but, it seems, I'd not sufficient breath –
the head grew, but a trunk, alas, was lacking.

Nature's fearful mysteries
hang in the air all about us.
Often it seems you understand them,
you're wound up, your eyes are bloodshot,
your hair's standing on end, your sinews strain.
But the moment passes, and again you stand and gape!

The happy plant enjoys its life,
like a child, playing in the open air.
But we who have torn our mad legs free,

run to and fro –
there is no joy in that.

Once I dug a small hole in the ground,
stuck one leg in, right up to the knee,
and stayed like that for fourteen days and nights.
I neither ate nor drank, grew thin,
and yet my leg did not take root.
Alas! I didn't turn into a plant.

However,
there's still much that I can sense.
Sometimes, pressing my ear to a birch trunk,
I can make out its quiet speech.
The birch passes on the fruit of its experience,
teaching me how to manage branches,
how to transfer the roots after a storm,
and how from my very self to grow.

And so, it you think I've learnt a lot,
and have earned the right to meditate on higher things,
think again! The beasts around me
curse, place obstacles in my path
and do not let me stand apart.
Strange creatures! They've no sense,
wanting to throttle cows, beat up bulls,
and whoever lives differently from them,
they slander and make fun of!

But nothing will persuade me to renounce
what I have learnt, even if,
in the process, I'll have turned mouse-grey.
Four times my experiments have sunk me.
For instance, once, quite unintentionally,
I set fire to myself –
my hind quarters were singed, but I survived…

Now there's one more feat I must attempt,
and there – I'll make no secret of it –
I'm ready to lay down my life,
to close my eyes, to return to the soil.

Neither death nor this earth can scare
one who has seen the stars shine,
who can commune with plants,
who understands how thought itself is formed.

So, be with me, my greatness! Sustain me!
I have grown like an oak, like a bull,
my bones are iron; now silver-haired,
I am prepared to carry out the deed.
Look! My head is shining,
my sinews strain, close to bursting.
Now I shall climb the mountain,
and thrusting with my legs, leap up.
With clawing hands, I'll clutch the air,
lift myself, then leap again, and again clutch.
And rising higher and higher,
soon, like a little bird, I'll fly, I'll fly!

I understand the atmosphere!
My belly fills with air, like a balloon.
The pressure of my arms won't yield to space.
By force of will I'll master it.

Paltry creature, worm in a mangy suit,
woodland tramp in a dunce's cap,
I am the king, the gladiator of the spirit,
a Harpagon, raised heavenward!

Birch trees, farewell, I'm leaving.
Like God I lived and saw no grieving.

3 GATHERING OF THE BEASTS

Chairman
Today is the anniversary of the Mad One's death.
Let us honour his memory.

Wolves
[singing]
Children, how terrible is this year.

The vault has descended on our lair.

Ancient beams are splintering.
Fluffy birds are twittering.

A storm-uprooted oak tree moans.
The wolf, struck in the belly, groans.

Two streams, abandoning their beds,
have flooded out a hundred dens.

Rise, beasts, all together come,
strike the basin, beat the drum.

The shadow of the The Mad One floats
like a whale in storm clouds cloaked.

Drenched in blood his lupine head,
grass is growing on his breast.

His paws are twisted to one side.
Smoke issues from his staring eyes.

Blow a blast upon the horn:
'Who are you, dread one forlorn?'

'I'm the Builder. The Axe am I.
Your holes and burrows are our prize.'

 Chairman
The night, which in this song
the poets have described,
I well recall.
From distant tundras, a storm arrived,
tearing the tops off oaks, capsizing stumps
and turning trees upside down.
The forest lost its head,
vaults cracked,
beams flew at us.
A ball of lightning, like a huge saucepan,
trundled down, crashing through the leaves,

and a tree flared, like a candle.
It screamed a horrid, feral scream,
waved its branches, begged for help.
And we who stood below, before it,
froze and could not lift a finger.

I ran. And there, ahead of me,
loomed a tremendous cliff,
its top smooth as a skull,
lovely in the drifting smoke.

Again the lightning coursed. Again I froze.
Above, on the very summit, I could just make out
a figure that ran about,
clutching the air.

I bellowed something. It leapt up,
a fearful howl transfixed me.
Arms, legs, a snout flashed in the air...
And that is all I can remember..

By morning, the storm had passed,
but the forest's ruins smouldered.
And I came to. The cliff still smoked,
and the Mad One's corpse lay on the pebbly strand.

    Student Wolf
Most honoured chairman, all of us lament
the Mad One's sad, untimely death.
But I've been delegated
to seek your answer to a question,
formulated by our board of students.

    Chairman
Speak.

    Student Wolf
Thank you. My question's plain.
We all know that the old forest's dead,
and that no boring mysteries remain
for us to believe in to the very end.

We are building a new forest, such as
has not been seen before on earth.
Men, women, children, all of us –
and I swear we shall complete the work.

Before your very eyes, we're altering
the universe, a wretched thing till now.
We sit before you on this day of reckoning,
engineers, judges, doctors, in a solemn row.

Mighty science sparkles like a water-spout.
The wolf eats pies and writes down figures.
He bangs in nails. The world trembles at his shout.
And our technical block's already finished.

And so, most honoured chairman, tell me,
why do you trouble our sobre world
with that apostate, traitor's crazy dreams?
The Mad One's plans are totally absurd!

Just ask yourself this. Can a plant be turned,
simply by dreaming, into an animal,
or a mere product of the earth
learn how to fly and then become immortal?

The dreams of the Mad One were crazy from the start.
He gave his life for them. Well, what of it!
The new century's song is ringing out.
We build a world, but you, you fly from it!

    Wolf Engineers
Arranging cross-beams in a special way,
we are throwing a bridge over to the other shores of animal
    felicity.
We are constructing electrical men,
who will bake pies.
Internal-combustion horses
will carry us across the bridge of suffering.
And a coachman in a glass hat
will sing a ditty: ,
      'Giddyup, gee-gee,

twice the ener-gee-gee!'
Of this sort is the builders' dream,
so their progeny should reign supreme.

Wolf Doctors
We, doctors, physicians,
interpreters of the beasts' emissions,
into the skulls of wolves insert glass tubes,
observe the brain at work, constructing,
the patient's coiffure not obstructing.

Wolf Musicians
On the body's violins, we
squeak, as science hath decreed.
With our noses' bow we saw
through the new days' bolted door.

Chairman
Slowly, slowly, slowly,
the marvellous age approaches.

Like balls of thread, we roll into the distance,
trailing our deeds behind us.
For we have woven wondrous cloth
and countless miles our feet have trod.

The forest, with its hunger, ill-hap, grief,
like a fiery neighbour, looms far off.

Look, beasts, at these woods. A bear
in them consumes a mare,
while we who dine on pies and ale
forget the caverns whence we hail.

Look, beasts, at this valley deep.
Consumed by beasts, a bullock weeps,
while we who have built our habitation
note down the magical equation.

Look at this world, oh valiant beasts.
Here the naked creatures course,

while we, with the sword of science unsheathed
to cut all evil off, go forth!

Slowly, slowly, slowly,
the marvellous age approaches.

I close my eyes and see a glass structure in the forest.
Handsome wolves, in lightweight clothing,
are engaged in long discussions on science.
One of them leaves the group,
lifts his limpid paws,
rises smoothly into the air,
lies on his back.
The wind propels this floater eastwards.
Below, the wolves are talking:
'Our philosopher has gone
to instruct the Burdock
in etherial geometry.'

What's this? Strange visions,
the soul's mad fabrication,
or simply the product of the mind?
Learned scholar, you decide!

The Mad One's dreams are quite absurd,
but you don't need eyes in the back of your head
to see that from the viewpoint of the old world
we're mad as hatters to be baking bread!

The ages pass, years drift away,
but living things are no dream;
they live and, living, they prevail
over the old truth's stern regime.

Sleep, Mad One, in your noble grave!
May your head, unhinged by its thoughts, rest now!
You do not know who dragged you from your den,
who harried you into a life of solitude and suffering.
Seeing nothing ahead, hoping for nothing,
you roamed the earth, like a great captain of thought.

Yours is the first breaking of the chains!
You are the river that gave birth to us!
We stand at the frontier of the ages,
workers, our heads like hammers.
We have sealed the ancient graveyard of the forest
with your mangled, rotted corpse.

Lie now in your grave, at peace,
Great Flyer, Great Topsy-Turvy.
We wolves will carry on your work,
your eternal labours. Onward to the stars!

[1931]

The Trees

Bombeyev
Who are you that nod your little heads,
playing with beetle and with ladybird?

Voices
– I am the solar power of leaves,
– I am the flower's stomach.
– I am the pistil's chandelier.
– I am the stem of humble stock.
– I am the little root of fate.
– And I'm tranquility's burdock.
– All together, we represent a flower,
its shoot, its tendrils' progress, hour by hour.

Bombeyev
And who are you, in the lakeland of the skies,
stretched out full length before our eyes.

Voices
– I am the ample contours of a cloud.
– I am the gustiness of wind.
– I am steam, rising from the body of a man.
– I am a drop of small span.
– I am smoke that's flown the coop.
– And I am animal soup.

Together, we're a storm of many volts,
a meet of thunderclaps and slumbering lightning-bolts.

Bombeyev
And who are you, like filaments and blobs,

demurely seated underneath the shrubs?

Voices
– We are the beetle's tiny eyes.
– I'm the caterpillar's snout.
– I am the seeded oats that sprout.
– I, the incipient soul's flageolet.
– We are viscera, with no body yet.
– I'm what will be the organ of breathing.
– I am the micro-organism's dream.
– I'm the candle's flickering.
– I am eyes opening on the earth's surface.
– And we are ciphers.
– Together, we compose a wonderful gestation,
the birth of everything, including your own nation!

Bombeyev
So long as nature draws me with its mysteries,
and propels me forward from behind,
I'll defy fate, and seek and find
my fathers, brothers, and my sisters.

1. INVITATION TO THE FEAST

The table was laid, and dinner
was set before us, broth of ox a'simmer,
and a hundred goblets, end to end,
circled the cauldron, like a hundred friends.
Bombeyev went out onto the porch,
lifted his face, shining like a torch,
and pointing to where groves sprang,
spoke thus:

Bombeyev
You, trees, emperors of the air,
clothed in voluminous green mantles,
that cover the whole length of your bodies
in circles, stars, and coronets!
You, trees, ancient dames of space,
decked out with a multiplicity of floral cups,

embellished with white doves!
You, trees, soldiers of time,
bristling with spines,
solidly based, with your three-storeyed roots
and other immovable foundations!
Some of you, having reached the limits of your age,
rest swart faces on the very edge of the atmosphere,
reminding me of fortified defences,
raised by nature, signifying power.
Others, not so lofty, but on the other hand more gracious,
celebrate wooden nuptials by night,
that nature might always and forever prosper
and everywhere her glory be proclaimed.
Finally, you, samovar trees,
filling your wooden interiors
with water from subterranean wells!
You, steamer-trees,
cleaving space, navigating
by means of a wooden compass!
You, cello trees and pipe trees,
jolting the air with your percussive notes,
composing tunes for forest and grove,
and plants that stand on their own!
You, axe-trees,
sectioning the air, then reassembling it,
in the name of a permanent equilibrium!
You, staircase-trees,
for the ascent of animals
into the furthest reaches of the air!
You, fountain-trees and explosion-trees,
battle-trees and sepulchre-trees,
trees as equilateral triangles and trees as spheres,
and all the other trees, whose names
do not submit to the laws of human language –
I say to you:
Welcome!

2. FEAST IN BOMBEYEV'S HOME

The forest hall gleams like an icon-lamp,
in a colonnade the graceful idols stand,
and the table's laid; the melodies resound,
and at the table sits the forest crowd.
Where young ladies perched on crimson velvets,
a crusty oak-tree, shower-fresh, now sits,
and a Greek chair, where Zina
gathered up her hair, admiring the flowing locks,
now sags: upon it sits an aspen,
with cuckoos and sparrows fully stocked.
And Bombeyev himself, among these splendid sofas,
is seated on his own; his gaze is sombre,
and over his lofty shoulders tumble curls –
his words are almost too faint to be heard.

    Bombeyev
Trees, listen to these words of mine,
which like an oven are raised before your eyes,
word upon word, as a mason plies his trade.
Let him be praised who peers inside,
as also the one who, in this stony land, discovers
that he himself grows wiser teaching others.

Trees, I'll compare the whole of nature to
an oven, its sturdy shoulders you,
you, its stout ribs, also its stoney breast,
you its whisperers with goodly heads,
emperors with shaggy, eagle pets,
time's soldiery that sets out on a trek!
But on the edge of nature, on the frontier
of the bright, the dull, the living, and the dead,
the plants' little countenances bloom
and like a drift of smoke, the grasses spread.
Tangled clumps, slender pipes uncouth,
umbels, into which glue's been poured,
tendrils, ugly and deformed,
creeping out through cracks, through pores,
and through the little windows of the universe
in an abundant, frothy turbulence.

Trees, listen to these words of mine
about the cow. She plods along,
an ambulent cliff, her muzzle
split by a crimson smile. But why
does this lumpish creature seem
so familiar to you and me?
The archaic cone of stony hooves,
the belly swaying at each step,
her two eyes swivelling wildly to the left,
she's dull, insensate, half alive?
Is she a mother? Perhaps we once
were curled up in this body, like her young?
Perhaps, pressing against her udder,
cheeks inflating like balloons, we shuddered?
And the mother-murderess's big teeth tore
the flowers and she munched them without shame,
and together with this mother we became
brute murderers of plants for evermore?

Trees, listen to these words of mine –
What's he like, the butcher?
A raised sword, his cleaver shines,
and murder's long been his familiar.
The cows' flanks still bulge with greenery,
but blood is billowing from her body,
and with blank eyes, the head
is flying through the air, and the dead cow
is lying in the dust, fit only for the pot –
her muscles scarcely even twitch.
But life's oven blazes on and on,
that which is elemental burns and spits,
and man adds sparkling crystals to the broth.
The beasts vanish, passing through our gut,
animals, vegetables, flowers,
and life's bulging oven doors are shut
to our ideas…
But what is this? Voices, I hear!

    Zina
Look, how the strip of sunset flares!

Bombeyev
On the porch, the forest warden's standing.

Zina
The trees are sobbing now in fear and trembling.

Forest Warden
I lived in the forest, in a lodge,
branded the trees with numbers,
and suddenly Bombeyev, on its edge,
sounded the woodland trumpet.
Plunging their elongated heads
in the clouds, the trees
hurtled into the fields. Ahead,
a world of chaos reeled.
Bombeyev, what right did you invoke
to scorn my order
and abduct the oak?

Bombeyev
Here it's I, not you, who am the master,
we can do without your order:
in it one notes the terrible traits of cannibalism.

Forest Warden
Why does cannibalism so distress you!
Seated at the table, clothed and fed,
aren't you yourself a cannibal, my friend?

Bombeyev
I am! A cannibal, and worse, a sinner!
Here lies the ox, the leavings of my dinner.
But now I swear, on his boiled head,
that this brigandage shall end
and my distant progeny will bring
to every household a new order of things.

Forest Warden
But has it occurred to you that,
in this golden age of yours, each gnat
that lays its daily hundred eggs must devour
you yourself, the garden, and every flower?

Bombeyev

According to his gnattish book of rules,
the gnat is acting on the loftiest priciples.

Forest Warden

So, putting on a splendid feast,
you've summed up all the world, I see,
grasped the movements of the spheres,
the procreation of the stars,
yet regularity hereunder
for you is simply a conundrum.
No, Bombeyev, you're mistaken,
major-general of thought!
It's a slanderous accusation
to say that our world has been bought!
In your mind, you have determined
that your life and you are vermin,
that, as you gobble down your food,
you're a cannibal, no good.
Man's an edifice of birds,
a receptacle of hairy beasts,
faces in his face interred
of the winged and quadruped.
And in him there dwell many creatures,
many fish that fled in vain,
but all in the light of consciousness
build the mansion of his brain.
Through mouth, oesophagus and stomach,
through the intestinal dungeon lies
nature's transcendental culvert
to the beatific mind.
So, long live the struggle,
the roar of beasts and crash of guns,
transformation of the living,
many consciousnesses made one!
And in this everlasting battle,
I, a man, unknown, unnamed,
proclaim a simple, universal,
honest, solid, wooden age.
I proclaim a glorious age
of lofty trees and mighty plains,

cool mountains, rivers loud,
a roseate sun among the clouds.
And may humans long continue
to speak of better years to come.
Trees, nature summons you,
as do the simple forest folk
and everything that lives, I see,
irrespective of its sort,
beneath the woodland wisdom's vault,
where the pine and beetle talk
and death, with springtime, is no more –
      Follow me!

3. NIGHT IN THE FOREST

Again, the misty trees; far off,
Bombeyev's house, like a little samovar...
The forest life continues, as before,
except that its work grows more complex.
The emperor-trees remove their crowns,
hanging them on the boughs,
and the rotation of wooden planets
round the denuded crowns begins.
The soldier-trees, clambering over one another,
form hollows, fortresses, obstructions,
crack their arms against the hard wood,
sound their trumpets, throw dice.
Here and there wooden girls
peep out from a gully –
their laughter resembles a dry pattering,
the crunch of twigs as a squirrel bounds along.
Then the cello-trees step forward,
coffers of strings wrapped in notes,
a moment later, the forest is girdled with pipes of lucent melody,
bordered by channels of song from the woodland orchestra.
Whether butterflies laugh, or bombs explode,
the song spreads and spreads.
And now, already, axe-trees cleave the air,
laying it out in even parallelograms.
The friction rouses various animals.

They set their dainty paws upon the stairs,
clambering towards the flat tops of the trees,
and remain there, motionless before the stars.
So, above the earth, a new plane is created:
below are animals, grasping the trees,
above, just the vertical stars.
But the earth does not fall silent. Already wooden girls
are dancing, raining mushrooms onto an ant-hill.
Just above them, tree-fountains take off,
huge vessels spurting into the air.
Beyond stand battle-trees and sepulchre-trees,
their foliage swollen, like bas-reliefs.
Here you may see Orpheus risen again,
playing on his pipe. The woodland beasts
take the singer to their chaste, leafy breast.
So, history lifts its head in the very midst
of the old, green woods, the bushes, pits and gullies.
So, the ancient chronicles are written,
shackled in the leaves and long boughs.
Further on, the trees lose their contours,
appearing now triangular, now semi-circular –
these are already abstract concepts.
Here, the Sphere Tree reigns over the others.
The Sphere Tree is a sign of the infinite tree,
the sum of all numerical operations.
Mind, do not look for it among the trees:
it is among them, and to the side, both here,
          and everywhere.

[1933]

translated by Robin Milner-Gulland

The Birds

If you would learn how the dove is made, how constructed –
   what veins
are within it, its wings how arranged, how its legs,
how its organs are disposed and, marvellously suspended
form a threefold shape in the frame of its bones –
first you must seek out a board; then with a keen plane
smooth down the surface completely, rub it with oil,
put it to hang in the wind, so that into the pores of the wood
the oil should thoroughly soak and remove any roughness.
After that, pupil, your instruments must be made ready:
wax-bottomed bath, cup full of transparent water,
bag of sharp pins, whipcord, balance with weights;
wash your hands well and report to me when you are ready

Birds, heaven's populace, hermits of air!
Singing passerines, thrushes, nightingales, linnets!
Put down your flutes, that's enough of your whistling and
   clicking.
Yes, and you come away from your organ-pipes, woodpecker.
You're an old organist, I know your tricks,
how with your bill you drum upon dry boughs:
the instrument throbs and vibrates, and the shattering notes
carry on wind through the whole of the neighbouring woodland.
Then, as I know, you select a bough somewhat longer;
a thinner sound is produced; a third thunders like a simandron.
O, wooden music of old untouched forests!
Creation's first converse, cradle of man's own speech.

Woodpecker, be you my witness, and you, musicians,
I've no quarrel with birds, nor am guilty of bloodshed.
Meagre my intellect, nailed by my feet to the earth;

unlike you, splendid birds, who can sweep through the air.
A hawk I'd gladly have been – but my hands are too feeble;
a falcon I'd gladly have been – but I cannot fly;
an eagle – but where the beak of an eagle should be
only my soft mouth stirs in a tousled beard.
Birds – open my eyes! Birds – tell me whence
you appeared? What riddle you carry within you?
How to decipher the time of the secretive cuckoo,
raven's alphabet, dove's arithmetic and heraldry?

Pupil, do as I say. Get your board ready.
Turn the dove onto its back with one hand. Its flight-feathers
must be pulled upwards, fastened with screws to the board,
so that the tips of wings reach up to the corners.
Then take two bits of cord, knot running loops in them,
put the loops over the feet and tie the ends to the free
lower corners – only make sure that the cord
is stretched as tight as can be, and the body is stable.

Here, then, before us it lies: a dove, a bird of the heavens,
haunter of steeples, inhabitant of wooden rafters;
having, at either side, wings of pure blue,
and a subtly-gleaming halo crowning its head.
Don't be afraid, but (plunging your hand in the vessel)
pluck off the feathers and down from its breast and its belly;
when you've done that, with your scalpel make an incision
right in the middle, where the long breastbone rises.
Splendid the keel of a ship, powerfully-sharp through the water,
strongly constructed by man to serve his own purpose!
How should we even begin to praise that marvel of lightness
the small breastbone of the dove, model for human endeavour?

All right lad, bring me your board. But what's going on?
You've gone pale, you've rushed to the window. Whose cries
do I hear in the wind? Louder and louder they grow.
Birds! birds flying this way! the sky is almost exploding,
cleft with hundreds of wings. The sun itself is eclipsed;
the roof's beginning to dance: the birds are on it – while others
are getting into the chimney. Yet others beat at the glass,
show me their bills, crush at the pane, clamber
onto each other, thrashing, calling, breaking the latch.
Birds! that's enough! Keep off I tell you! just wait!

Magpie, go to the devil! – you're always trying
to push to the front. Stop banging your beak for a moment!
Stop all that noise on the glass. You'll break it, and find
it hard to replace. Come on, bird, get out of the way,
no more playing the fool. You, long-billed herons,
you move away. That's better. Just take your hands off me, crow!
You'll get such a dusting-down you'll be cawing like crazy
for weeks. That's the window open at last.

Well then, come along quick! Here are your seats and your
    benches.
Smaller ones, warblers, jays, robin-redbreasts,
you sit in front, to see what's going on. Crows and woodpeckers,
owls, hawks, sit behind them. Capercailzie can sit
on the backs of the chairs. Bluetit, you on the candlestick;
chaffinch, you on the clock (but don't touch the hands!). We
    shall have to
move the screen forward a bit, or the cuckoo and nightingale
won't have a place to sit. Magpie, quiet with the lamp!
Glitter it may, but you won't drag it off to your nest.
Quiet now, everyone. Time to get on with our work.

Strange is the huddle of organs which we now glimpse:
pipes, branches, sacks; some reddish, while some
are deep blue, some translucent. Among them, most delicate
    membranes
are everywhere stretched. Search out, pupil, a piece
of glass tube, thrust it into the opening of the trachea,
carefully blow. You see how the transparent membranes
swell like balloons. Very well now, birds, tell me
how do you breathe when in flight? whence comes the air you
    inhale?
If you had no such air-bags within you, surely
would you not gasp for breath in the wind up aloft?

We must divide ourselves now into three smaller groups.
The woodpecker will be the first group's leader. The
    mocking-bird
will be the second's, the heron the third's. Look, woodpecker:
the pale-blue thing in this bag is the heart. Take some scissors
in your black claws, and snip through the bag. Now you see –
there is the heart! Mocking-bird, you must remove

the red liver, and after – the spleen. Now from the belly
the crop must be drawn out, with gullet, intestines and stomach,
and, when dissected and washed, in the wax-bottomed bath
be secured firmly with pins. Where's the long-billed heron?
You, heron, busy yourself with the brain. Go on – hold the head
    tighter;
turn back the skin, and then take it off like a glove. Now look:
the bone has been bared. So it shouldn't get in the way,
it must be filed through. Easy enough. Well, begin.

So our work is now over. In front of us lie
the delicate bones, veins, organs and nerves of the dove
in a heap. Dissected with a sharp knife,
the dove is no longer a bird, and never again will it fly
onto the roof with its mate. Even were we to wish
once again to suspend organs from bones, and the veins
so to extend that the blood coursed along them again,
connect up the muscles as previously they were connected,
so that the body resumed its entire former shape – even then
the dove would not come back to life. Puny, man's hand:
that which once has been killed he cannot resurrect.

Could I assimilate this will of mine to the will
of Nature, my word to the visionary word,
could I envisage how all that I see – birds, animals, trees,
stones, rivers and lakes – were homogeneous limbs
of a single marvellous body, then, without doubt,
should I be the better creator, my reason not blunder –
striding the highroad of truth. Benighted my science;
yet even now something speaks of the mighty chain
of creation, where all metamorphoses are directed
to a single wise end: that old, worn-out forms
should be recast into vessels of more perfect aspect.

Sit down at table now, birds. We're going to have supper. Eat up
the remains of the dove, crows! what once cooed up above
can be put to good use. You, yellow-hammers and quails,
can peck at some meal – here you are. For the others
here's a trug full of worms and a bowl of caterpillars.
See how they wriggle? These ones with a furry back –
they're very tasty. As for those sausage-shaped ones,
threads are strung through them in various places. And these

put out long horns in front; while some describe a tall arc
standing quite firm on their heads and their tails.
Splendid creatures they are! Peck at them, chop them and rip them!

But for us, pupil, bring the fat meat of the cow:
boiled to perfection, and giving an excellent soup.
Cut me some bread, grate some onion onto the plate,
put out pepper, to warm my insides in an instant.
I nearly forgot! Would you look on the shelf by my mortar:
there's a grey bag, and in it should still be
an old bunch of garlic. There is? Bring it out, lad.
That head for you, this for me…let's begin.

A quiet sunset hangs over the earth. Reddish patches
stretch from window to floor. Nature's mysterious rest
is near. Would you open the door, lad, and give me
my evening hat from the peg? Greetings, bright evening,
evening of life, my old age! Very soon shall I too
lie down and rest, and above my permanent bed
may clouds swim, and birds fly, and the planets
follow their course. Birds, the closer my hour draws
the more do I love you. Small sons of the Universe,
scraps, aerial fauna, fragments of animal life,
drawn into the sky – why do you keep such a troubled
gaze fixed upon me? No answer? Let's go outside
together and watch the sun go down to its rest.

Off with you, children. Beyond the great darkening forest
the bright sun has set. From over the rim of the world
its rays just reach to the clouds. The tops of the evening trees
stand against their red glow. Golden figures of clouds
undulate gently, and changing from shape to shape
slowly move through the sky. There's the head of a giant,
there – an aerial horse. Beyond it, three clouds fused together
take up the form of Laocoon. There by the forest
rides a cloud-horseman; the wind is removing
head from right arm, and bearing it off to the West.

Evening, I welcome you. Ponderous herons and woodpeckers
stride along next to me, full of importance. The quail,
warblers and yellow-hammers dart by in flocks, now descending,
now rising again, and in the air over my head

twitter gaily. The robin, abandoning the flock,
suddenly sits on my shoulder and leans his soft head
on my cheek. Funny fellow, what is it? Maybe
you've something to tell me? No? Look at the sky:
see how the clouds hurry past? You and I, lad,
are also perhaps two clouds, only one has a beard,
and one a light wing – growing into eternity both.

Here's the end of our path. We have climbed a green hillock
and shall not go further. The narrow edge of the sun
can from here still be seen. Well, children, goodbye.
Time to sleep, time to sleep. Tomorrow a marvellous morning
will rise on the earth, and the sun, washed with dew,
will look into your nests, and, with a delicate ray,
open your clear eyes. And there one flock rises,
with a rustle of wings and a cry it departs for the forest,
saying farewell to me. Thereupon rises another
up from under my feet. Farewell! And a third
leaps from the earth, detaches itself into air. Further,
further the birds fly, and the sun's angled rays
inundate flock after flock, paint them rosy.

Only the robin-redbreast remains. Silly bird!
What have you lingered behind for? Hop into my hands!
Don't you see night is approaching? Humans too
are going to sleep – some on beds, some in haylofts.
Animals go to their lairs, cows slumber in stalls.
Past the houses walks Sleep, glances into the windows, keeps
    looking:
'Who's still awake? He'll be for it!' The watchman
bangs on his sounding-board. How about this? –
I'll stretch out my hand, you take off from my palm, and you'll
    quickly
catch up the flock. All right? Fly away! And he's flown.

Sleep walks past the houses. Earth, mother mine, I shall lie –
soon shall I too lie down in your depths. Then, as if to a child,
tell me this tale. Sleep walks past the houses... still walks,
looks: 'Who's still awake? I'll give him what for!'... Only these,
only these words are needed, not another word more.

[1933]

Pre-imprisonment Poems

THE FACE OF A HORSE

Animals do not sleep. In the dark of night,
they stand, a wall of stone, above the world.

The cow's sloping head
rustles the straw with its smooth horns,
the rocky brow a wedge between age-old cheekbones,
the mute eyes revolving sluggishly.

The horse's face is handsomer, more knowing.
He hears the murmur of leaves and stones,
and, attentive to the wild beast's cry,
hears, too, the nightingale's gurgle in the copse.

And knowing all, to whom may he recount
his wondrous visions?
Cimmerian darkness!
Over the skyline, constellations rise.
The horse stands, like a knight on guard,
the wind plays in his hair,
his eyes burn, like two huge worlds,
his mane spreads, like the imperial purple.

And should a man but see
the horse's magic face,
he would tear out his own pathetic tongue
and give it to the horse. In truth,
this magic beast is worthy of it.

Then we would hear words.
Words, big like apples,
thick, like honey or curds,
words that penetrate like fire,
and once within the soul, as in some hut,
illuminate the wretched trappings,
words that will not die,
and which, in song, we celebrate...

But now the stable is empty,
the trees, too, have dispersed,

pinch-faced morning has swathed the hills,
opened the fields up for work.
And the horse, in its cage of shafts,
dragging a covered cart,
looks with submissive eyes
at the enigmatic, stationary world.

[1926]

translated by Robin Milner-Gulland

TREES

In our abodes
We live our lives by reason, not by beauty,
Marking their feastdays, born of humankind –
The trees elude us.

In truth the trees are solider than bronze
With their green glint of interlocking curls.

Some of them, rearing heads up to the heavens,
Seem to have hidden eyes within their crowns;
The battered charms of childish arms,
Clad in their muslin-foliage,
Have not yet had their fill of wholesome fruits
And keep the sonorous fruits in hand.

Thus through the centuries, through settlements, through
    gardens
There glimmer in our sight the wholesome fruits.

We cannot comprehend this beauty –
The humid respiration of the trees.
See how the woodmen, axes laid aside,
Stand and look on, quite still, without a word.
Who knows what thoughts have crossed their minds,
What memories and what discoveries,
Why, pressing to cold trunks
Their faces, they weep unrestrainedly?

Here we have found a new-formed glade,
Spring up at various points,
Grow tall and slender. Heads bump up
Against the heavens, which descend towards us.
Our flaccid flesh rigidifies,
Our veins have marvellously stiffened,
Our rooted feet no longer may be raised
Or outstretched arms be lowered.
Our eyes have closed, the flux of time grows sluggish,
Gently the sun reaches out for our heads.

Moist waves are coursing through our legs.
This moisture rises up and then fans out,
Bathing our foliage-faces:
It is the earth nurturing its new child;
While far away there billows over the town
A piercing wedge of lamplight.

The town's a little donkey, a four-walled house,
Trundling on a pair of stony wheels
—Its arid smokestacks all atilt —
Along the firm horizon.
The day was bright. And there were empty clouds
Floating like puckered bubbles.
A wind blew up. It riffled past the forest,
And there we stood, slim trees,
In a pale emptiness of skies.

[1926]

POPRISHCHIN[1]

When roads are frozen solid
and windblown crosses reel,
with frenzied fingers Gogol
leads out his hunchbacked dreams.
And by the bitter coldness,
by melancholy bled,
the stone-faced horror staggers,
and the wind aims at the head.
It tears men's cloaks from their shoulders,
exploding the ashen snows,
then by degrees sinking lower,
lies down to lick their toes.
From where does it get its power?
No longer a demon, but he –
Poprishchin, lifting his eyebrows,
turns his face from the lee.
Wind, whirl through the offices,
sweeping up quills in your path,
Spain rises to the occasion,
spreading its pearly fan.
It will flourish a purple mantilla
over its native fields,
and clamorous Seville in a body
will turn out to greet its king.
And he, now haggard and fleshless,
with a luminous, suffering gaze,
will rise up…
            A warden, a mattress,
a cot and darkness again.
The shirt digs into the armpit,
Medzhi[2] whining, pulls on the leash,
in the window's a hint of dawn…
Wind, irrupt in the offices,
pursue the snow down the street,
bury the carriages with their
glittering grandees.
Past windows, arches, porches,
past columns the tempest blows,
tears off the general's orders,

buries the bridges in snow.
It stretches its limbs, it rushes,
sounds an icy blast on the horn,
after it snow-fiends tumble,
racing over the roofs.
They grapple
the tall bell-towers,
exploding
the bells inside,
lie down in the slaughter-houses,
then again from a corner fly
to where, outstaring the blizzard,
making his last brave stand,
his white shirt billowing,
sways dead-faced
Ferdinand.

[1928]

1. Poprishchin is the character from Gogol's story 'Diary of a Madman', a poor clerk
   who imagines himself to be Ferdinand, King of Spain.
2. Medzhi is a dog belonging to the daughter of the director of the bureau where
   Poprishchin works. Poprishchin imagines himself to be in love with her.

AT THE FISHMONGER'S

Now forgetting the devious ways of men,
we enter a different domain…
Here's a sturgeon, rosy-fleshed,
the finest sturgeon of them all,
suspended now, with arms outstretched,
hooked through, hanging by the tail.
Below it, a salmon, meatlike, glows,
and eels resembling sausages,
in smoke-dried magnificence and sloth,
with knees tucked neatly in are steaming,
while in their midst, a yellow tusk,
His Grace the Cured Fillet's gleaming.

O, splendid autocrat of the belly,
god of the intestines and lord,
clandestine leader of my spirit,
architricline[1] of my thought,
I want you! Give yourself to me!
Let me gorge until I drop!
My mouth's on fire, quivering,
my guts tremble like Hottentots,
emotion-gripped, my stomach strains,
hunger releasing floods of juice –
now it stretches like a dragon,
now with all its force contracts –
mouthfuls of saliva sluice,
muttering, through gritted teeth!
I want you! Give yourself to me!

Cans are clattering all over,
white fish howl and take the plunge,
knives stand up on end from gashes,
tinkling a little as they lunge;
the fish tank's glow is submarine,
where, behind its glassy walls,
bream swim in a delirium,
hallucinated, bored –
filled with doubt or maybe fear?
Death looms like a costermonger,
brandishing a bronze fish-spear.

Scales are reading the 'Our Father',
two weights sit calmly in a pan,
determining the course of life.
A door rings out, fish squirm and flap,
and gills suck air contrarywise.

[1928]

1. Architricline: ruler of a feast, in ancient Rome.

IMMORTALITY

Cats on the springy staircase lifting
their broad kissers, as they sit
on the banisters like buddhas,
sound off, trumpeting their love.
Naked kitties, in a throng,
apologizing, rub along.
Coquettes! How they abound,
sideways on, and round and round,
flowing with amatory juice,
trembling, filling the whole house
with the scent of passion. Cats
scream, their jaws unbattened;
they are like devils, roosting there
in their coats of silvery fur.

One cat, in this foreign land,
muses for now and doesn't chant.
Busy with their round-dance, flees
caper in his matted fleece.
Hermit of the dismal staircase,
ascetic of the slop pail, monk,
by him the primary world's contained
in cerebral pits and bumps.
Through the door he senses the apartment,
where the days's work's scarcely started,
where, between the stove and toilet,
gallop only female torsos;
the primus, like a torture rack,
is set out, crackling upon it,
a shocked fish howls consumptively,
covered in glaucous, greasy blotches;
there, scrubbed animal cadavers
sprawl limply over unlit griddles,
and vessels, cast-iron fonts of weeping,
crown the apotheosis of evil.

The cat rises, quivering,
clearly the world has been excluded,
and only slops are splashing where

wisdom's effigy once brooded.
And the cat rises on his hind legs,
advances, with his paws held high,
the stairs have vanished. Too dark
to see. The women shy –
it's late! Landing on her neck,
the cat writhes like a devil, rends
the body, opens up the veins,
savagely claws out the bones...
O, God, God, how absurd!
Has he gone blind, or is he mad?

Night, without bitterness or dread,
passed; it was strange to contemplate
that yard, where the cat met his fate,
the moon lifting slowly overhead.
In unison, trees swayed with grace,
disporting their large, solid frames,
naked birdies chirped and preened,
hopping on unsteady pins
above them, baring one yellow fang,
the cat's enormous carcass hung.

Bait for crows, you have become!
Monk, farewell... In my window,
pursuing their wild carnival,
she-cats once more race to and fro.
And I am standing on the stairs,
as radiant and majestic,
continuing your life up there,
my gallant, righteous fellow.

[1928]

SICKNESS

Helpless on his bed, the sick man
can't so much as lift a hand.
His sweaty brow a rectangle,
a fortnight he has lain there ill.
In his dreams there pass before him
faces, oaken and obtuse.
Here a horse half raises its eyelid,
displaying a quadrangular tooth.
It champs on empty phials and tubes,
leans over, reads the Testament,
dances, urinates into a tub,
and in his wife's voice soothes the sick man.

'Wife, you were supposed to be a girl!
Dear friend, alas –
how supple was the tender skin
of your flanks.
Why have you become a horse?
Get thee to a white monastery,
and to god dedicate a candle –
and then bite through your bridle!'

But the horse shrugs and doesn't move.
On the contrary, it is content.
Already evening has arrived,
and light onto the table is shed.
In the yard, a priest appears,
cursing and straining every nerve,
the cast-iron crucifix of silver
with verve he hauls across the porch.
The man feels better. The priest guffaws,
in holy vestments wholly wrapped,
sprinkles the patient with his aspergillum,
then from the plate he grabs
a barleymeal-stuffed rennet-bag,
and mama is what he calls the nag.

[1928]

translated by Robin Milner-Gulland

DINNER

We shall unbend our weary bodies.
A splendid evening melts beyond the window.
So pleasant to prepare a meal:
the bloodstained art of living!

Little potatoes rush around the pan,
wagging their childish heads;
a purple slug of meat has been suspended,
so heavy and so clammy, that
the pallid water scarcely can contain it –
it slowly bubbles and goes gently pink;
the meat then settles horizontally
and sinks down naked to the bottom.

Out race the onion-bulbs,
transparent peel asqueak,
and suddenly disrobing, they
glitter in splendid nudity;
here a plump carrot stirs
and falls in circlets on a dish;
there cunning celery conceals itself,
crowned delicately with curls;
massive as the Atlantic sways
the turnip's firm planed breast.

A splendid evening melts beyond the window,
yet daylight shines forth from the vegetables.
We'll take them up in placid hands,
wash them with pallid water:
they will be warmed within our palms,
then slowly sink below.
The primus-stove, our stumpy household dwarf,
will flare forth in a tinkling halo.

And this is death. If we could only see
no more these city-squares, no more these walls –
rather the tepid innards of the earth

warmed through with vernal languour;
if only we could see in shining rays
the blissful childhood of the plants –
surely we should descend upon our knees
before the bubbling pan of vegetables.

[1929]

A WALK

The animals have no names –
who said they should be given any?
Suffering without end
is their hidden destiny.
The bull moves off into the pastures,
talking with nature as he goes,
over lovely eyes are planted
alabaster horns.
Lying quietly in the meadows,
like a simple country girl,
the stream now laughs out loud, now sorrows,
thrusting limbs into the earth.
Why is she so melancholic?
What is it that ails,
the whole of nature smiling,
like a cheerless cell?
In the field each tiny flower
gestures, fluttering its hand.
The great bull, grey tears flowing,
superb yet scarcely living, stands.
A bird circles weightlessly
in the deserted air, alone,
its small voice labouring
over an old tune.
Before it, waters sparkle,
and the vast woodlands sway,
nature, with its laughter,
dies each moment of the day.

[1929]

SNAKES

The forest murmurs, swaying,
and the different flowers nod,
reptile bodies, glittering,
lie coiled among the rocks.
The sun, so hot and simple,
pours its warming rays on them.
Among the rocks their bodies,
gleaming smooth, like glass, are strewn.
If a bird cries out above them,
or a bug howls boldly past,
the snakes sleep, faces hidden
in baking, glossy folds.
Indigent and enigmatic,
there they slumber, mouth ajar,
while above them, scarcely noticed,
time drifts by upon the air.
One year passes, and another,
three years pass, and finally
a man comes on these bodies,
weighty images of sleep.
What is their origin, their purpose,
can they be justified?
In their heaps, the lovely creatures
sleep, scattered on every side?
The philosopher departs now,
avoiding his fellow men,
and nature, losing interest,
stands above him like a cell.

[1929]

TEMPTATION

Death comes to a man. 'Good sir,'
he says, 'I'd have you know,
you're no better than a cripple,
bit by fleas from head to toe.
Follow me, give up this life,
it's peaceful in my cemetery.
Every person, great and small,
I swaddle in a winding-sheet.
Don't complain, you'll leave a gap,
that all your science will die with you:
fields will turn themselves, my friend,
rye spring up without a plough.
The sun may scorch at noon,
but by dusk it has turned tail.
Schooled by long experience, you'll
slumber on, heroic, pale,
hugging a square crucifix,
in that made-to-measure pit.

'Death, don't touch! Hands off, I say,'
the peasant answers him in kind.
'Take pity, death, on my white hair,
and let me go just one more time.
Just give me a little extra.
Let me off the hook – I swear
I'll repay you for your trouble,
my daughter give into your care.'

Death, not laughing and not weeping,
puts his arms about the maid,
like a forest fire sweeping,
grasses bending low beneath him,
from the cottage to the gate.

A low mound stands above the grass,
within the mound the maiden cries:
'How hard to lie here in the grave,
my milky arms are black as pitch,
and my hair's a film of dust,

feather-grass grows from my breast.
How hard to lie here in the grave,
my tender lips have now decayed,
two ringlets have I where were eyes,
and no sweet lover by my side!'

Death laments and also hoots,
as he flies above the mound,
points his gun at it and shoots,
then exclaims, as he bends down:
'Enough of this, my little maid,
enough of bawling in the grave!
There are worlds beyond our world.
Take heart now, crawl out of your tomb!
The wind is stiffening in the field,
and the night is coming soon.
Caravans of dozing stars
have assembled and streaked by.
Your subterranean stint is done,
try a little harder, rise!'

The maiden cannot believe her ears,
wildly flails about her, hears
a board give. Up she leaps.
Crash! She's splitting at the seams!

And the poor thing oozes, oozes
tiny intestines, it seems.
Where before her blouse was,
a film of dust's all that remains.
From every opening of her body
timid worms are gazing coyly,
lapping up the pinkish balm,
little naked babes-in-arms.

Soup she is who was a maid.
Don't laugh, laughter! Just you wait!
The sun will rise, the clay will crack,
the risen maid is coming back.
From her shin-bone, there will spring
a sapling, bursting into song,

a song to celebrate the maid,
a tender song to celebrate:
'Hushaby, my little babe,
hushaby, my little maid!
From the field the wind has flown,
above it stands the pallid moon.
The peasants sleeping in their huts,
many kittens have they got.
And every kitty you see there,
each cat a crimson collar wears,
and a coat of blue-grey fur,
and a pair of golden boots,
and a pair of golden boots,
very precious, very rare...'

[1929]

SIGNS OF THE ZODIAC GROW DIMMER

Signs of the Zodiac grow dimmer
over the expanse of fields,
Dog, the animal, is dozing,
Sparrow bird is fast asleep.
Breasts as round and firm as turnips,
fat-bottomed mermaids fly,
limbs as stout as staves and sturdy,
heading straight into the sky.
On a triangle, a witch
turns into a puff of smoke,
with the wood-elves a deceased
nimbly dances the cakewalk.
After them, intoning palely,
wizards hunt the spritely Fly,
with the moon, immobile lately,
above the hilltops floating high.

Signs of the Zodiac grow dimmer
over village edifices,
Dog, the animal, is sleeping,

as also Plaice the fish is.
Clack–clack–clack, a rattle goes,
Spider's resting on his oars.
Cow is sleeping, Fly is too,
right above them hangs the moon.
Above the earth, a pan of water,
overturned, drifts in the skies.
A goblin from his shaggy beard
has plucked a beam… What a surprise!
From behind the clouds, a siren
pokes a sweet extremity,
a cannibal has gnawed a
gent's… O, where's his decency!
General revelry's the ticket,
while in all directions fly
large baboons and Britons, witches,
dead men and the smaller fry.

Candidate of ages past,
captain of what lies ahead,
O, my mind! These monstrous beings
folks can't get into their head.
In nature's crowded market-place,
indigent, besmeared with dirt,
what's the trouble, freedom's monarch,
restless ashes of the earth?

Lofty is its dwelling place…
Late! High time to settle down…
Mind, my wretched warrior,
you should slumber on till dawn.
Why have doubts, concerns? Be bold!
The day is gone, and you and I,
half creaturely and half divine,
fall asleep upon the threshold
of a different labouring life.

Clack–clack–clack, a rattle goes,
Spider's resting on his oars.
Cow is sleeping, Fly is too,
right above them hangs the moon.

Above the earth, a pan of water,
overturned, drifts in the skies.
Spud the vegetable slumbers.
Sleep now, reader, close your eyes!

[1929]

ART

A tree grows, recalling
a natural column of wood.
Limbs radiate, hung with round-faced leaves.
Trees, gathered thus,
make up a forest, verdant.
But to define a forest
by its formal structure only
is inadequate.

A cow's solid body,
set on four endings,
crowned with a temple-form headpiece,
two horns like the moon in its first quarter,
is also implausible,
unintelligible,
if we forget its significance
in the universal scheme of things.

A house, an edifice of wood,
like a tree-cemetery,
a cabin of corpses,
a gazebo of the dead –
what mortal eye can understand,
what living creature make sense of it,
if we forget the builder
and the one who felled the trees?

Man, sovereign of the planet,
ruler of the woodlands,
emperor of cattle flesh,
Sabaoth of the two-storeyed house,
he lords it over the planet,

he cuts down the forest,
he dismembers cattle –
but utter a word, he cannot!

Yet I, a faceless man,
held a long, gleaming flute to my lips,
blew, and obediently
words flew into the world and became objects.

The cow made porridge for me,
the tree read me a story,
and the world's dead little houses
jumped up and down, as if alive.

[1930]

STARS, ROSES, SQUARES, AND ARROWS

Stars, roses, squares, and arrows
of the Aurorora Borealis,
slender, striped, or circular,
overhung our edifices.
Staves and goblets, wheels revolving,
overhung our houses, in the
attics felines screaming,
telescopes on tripods rumbling.
But the goggle-eyed contraptions
swept the night sky to no purpose,
all the squares took off, the goblets
vanished, and the staves and arrows.
Only a little bird was left there,
between the sun and moon, located
in an opening of a cloudlet,
singing loud as it could manage:
'Hover not, you stars and roses,
fly away, you staves and goblets –
between the sun and moon, the morning
wanders off into the distance!'

[1930]

THE QUEEN FLY[1]

A grey cock flaps and preens,
night advances on all fronts.
Like a star, the Queen Fly swoops,
passing low across the swamps.
The framework of her body, bared,
thrums its little upright wings,
on her breast the pentagram
of wonders, wrought in rays of light.
On her breast's the pentagram,
between two glassy pinions,
like the primary symbol on
as yet undeciphered tombs.

There is a strange kind of moss,
fragile, pinkish, myriapod,
quite transparent, just alive,
even by the grass despised,
orphan, wondrous denizen
of remote, ill-favoured spots,
offering a place to live
to the hovering fly above.
Still vibrating brittle wings,
flexing its small pectorals,
the insect circles and descends
onto the tufa of the swamp.

If you're troubled by a dream,
you know the good word Elohim,
take this oddly favoured fly,
put the creature in a jar,
walk about the field with it,
pay attention to the signs.
If the insect barely murmurs,
copper's lying underfoot.
If it flutters its antennae,
it is telling you of silver.
But if it briskly beats its wings,
a pot of gold is buried there.

Softly, softly night arrives,

audible the poplars' scent.
My breath fades, it dies away
between the poplars and the fields.
The dismal marshes are asleep,
the roots of grasses are astir.
In the graveyard someone weeps,
pressing his body to a mound.
Someone moans, someone sobs,
stars cascading from above.
Moss is glimmering far off.
Fly, oh fly, where have you gone?

[1930]

1. Note by Zabolotsky: The Fly Queen, so called by the celebrated Agrippa von
   Nettesheim [1485–1536, his work on occult subjects earned him a reputation as a
   magician. – Trans.], refers to a certain mysterious insect the size of a large bumble-
   bee, which 'likes to settle on a water plant called *Fluteau Plantaginé*, and with the
   help of which, apparently, the Hindus search for buried treasure in their country.'

SAMOVAR

Samovar, sovereign of the belly,
household priest of high reknown!
In your breast an ear I see,
in your foot I see a brow.
Imperator of white teacups,
of pots of tea, archimandrite,
your throaty grumbling is replete
with all that evil can devise.
But I'm a maiden, innocent
as a flowering plant, untouched.
A slender stream of boiling water
sweetly pours into the cup.
And an infant room, entire,
held in distant focus then,
blooms like a forget-me-not,
on its tall and narrow stem.

[1930]

POEM OF THE RAIN

Wolf
Respected woodland snake, my dear,
why do you crawl, not knowing where
you're going, or why you're in
a hurry? Life's not for hurrying!

Snake
We do not find intelligible
a world that's always at a standstill.
And so, wise wolf, we run about,
like smoke escaping from a hut.

Wolf
It is not hard to get your drift –
the snake is not renowned for wit!
But you're running from yourself, my light,
if you suppose there's truth in flight.

Snake
You're an idealist, I see.

Wolf
Look, a leaf falls from a tree.
The cuckoo builds its song, it chimes
on two notes, simple-minded child,
the trees about it standing tall.
The sun shines and the clear rains fall,
the water flows for several seconds,
the barefoot peasant doesn't comment,
and after that it's bright again,
no drops are falling, there's no rain.
Tell me, what does this signify?

Snake
Go to the wolves, they'll tell you why
water falls on us from the sky.

Wolf
Fine. I'll address my wolfish ranks.

The water courses down their flanks.
The water sings out like a mother,
when it pours gently down upon us.
Nature, in a sarafan,
leans its head against the sun,
plays the organ day and night,
and we call this playing life.
And we call it rain, when through
puddles tramp the tiny tots,
the woods and thickets dance and sigh,
there's laughter of forget-me-nots.
Or, when the organ note of gloom
sounds, and above is heard a drum,
and a gigantic host on high
fills every corner of the sky.
When the waters' mighty flood
overturns the woodland creature,
in ourselves not yet believing,
we call the surging waters: God.

[1931]

THE SCHOOL OF BEETLES
[Fragment of a long poem]

Women

We, women, mistresses of the cauldron,
inventresses of porridge,
impellers of the world on,
day and night, day and night,
full of loving industry,
give birth to fat, red infants.
Like ships, putting out on a long voyage,
they come fully equipped with organs –
some for present use, others for later.
Mountains of complex, living flesh
we lay in mankind's arms.
You, carpenters, scholars of the forest,
you, stonemasons, builders of cabins,

you painters, covering walls
with enigmatic figures from our history, –
open the infant's eyes,
unstop his ears,
and encourage the untutored reason
in its first exploits.

Carpenters
We, carpenters, scholars of the forest,
mathematicians of the lives of trees,
will construct for the infants huge cradles
on stout oak legs.
Great seafarers
will be given beds of maple –
its fibre is knit
like the surf.
For weavers, engineers of clothing,
a bed of plane-wood is appropriate –
the plane's a weaver-tree,
weaving itself.
The ash, with its oblong clouds,
instructs us in aeronautics.
The dark stripes of the larch
teach the laying of rails.
The pear and lime are tutors to little girls.
The moabi resembles honey, advising bee-keepers.
The thuja, lord of groats, is a lesson to the farmer.
The brown nut-tree is like the earth, the navvy's mate.
Rosewood teaches stone-breaking and house-building.
Ebony is metal's double,
a light for smiths,
for generals and enlisted men an education.

Painters
We paint the shapes of beasts
and scenes from the lives of plants.
Instead of the Madonna,
a cow, reading a textbook on Butter Manufacturing,
will shine above the infant's bed.
We paint the dance of the camels
in the vast sands of Samarkand,

where a glass bowl
follows the sun's trajectory.
We paint
the history of new plants.
Offspring of simple gardeners,
they have filled out like bombs.
We shall not forget their first awakening,
when in the leaf's little foot a muscle started,
in the potato's body, the rudiment of a brain appeared,
and the maize's tiny eye
opened on the stalk's end.
We paint the warring of cereals,
the battle of oats and sparrows,
the day a bird fell,
slapped down by leaves.
This is what, in our paintings, we depict
Once seen, the memory of them
is carried to the grave.

.ſĭıııı ıııı ıııı

We shall erect a hundred statues of alabaster,
the tops of their heads sawn through,
brain gone, and into the smooth eye-sockets
rain water flowing,
so pigeons may besport themselves.
A hundred headless heroes
will stand there in the open,
holding the tops of their heads.
They have raised these stone caps from their skulls,
as if to salute the future!
A hundred observers of the lives of animals
have consented to offer up their brains
and to transfer them to the brain-boxes of asses,
so that the rational kingdom of the beasts may dawn.
This is mankind's voluntary settling of accounts
with its slaves!
The most awesome sacrifice
the stars have yet witnessed!
Henceforth, may the image of these heroes
inspire the world of infants.
These small citizens of the world

will play
at the stone feet of the statues,
will lob smooth pebbles
into the wise men's skulls,
will listen to the gurgle of water
the talk of pigeons,
in the stony bosom of the world
will discover beetles and grasshoppers.
Beetles with motionless wings,
embryos of renowned Socrateses,
form little balls of bread,
to make themselves wise.
Grasshoppers, entomological clocks,
keep track, calculating
how much time each has in which to develop his mind
and when to pass it on to his progeny.
Thus, travelling from one body to another,
mysterious reason grows.
The grasshopper's time and the beetle's space –
this is the infancy of the world.

    Women
We hear you,
carpenters, painters and stonemasons!
Now are the foundations laid
of the first School of Beetles.

[1931]

THE BATTLE OF THE ELEPHANTS

O warrior of the word, it is time
for your sword to sing out at night!

The horses of adjectives fling themselves upon
impotent little nouns,
shaggy knights
pursue the cavalry of verbs,
and shells of interjection
tear overhead, like signal rockets.

Battle of words! Meanings' clash!
The tower of Syntax, sacked.
The Europe of consciousness
in the flames of insurgency.
Despite the enemy guns,
raining down broken letters,
the warlike Elephants of the Subconscious
creep out like gigantic babes
and stamp their feet.

But now, having fasted since birth,
they hurl themselves into the secret breaches,
and with human figures between their teeth
rear happily on their hind legs.
Elephants of the Subconscious!
Militant beasts of the nether regions!
They stand and salute with merry thunder
all that has been got through plunder.

The Elephants' small eyes are crafty,
filled to the brim with joy and laughter.
So many toys! So many crackers!
Having tasted blood, the guns fall silent.
Syntax builds the wrong sorts of houses,
the world stands in its clumsy loveliness!
The old code of the trees discarded,
the battle directs them to new pastures.
They discuss and write, on literature bent,
the world is filled with awkward content.
The wolf has fitted a human face

over his own battered snout,
he produces a flute, wordlessly plays
the warlike Elephants' first lays.

Poetry, having lost the battle,
stands limply in its tattered crown.
Centennial Mont-Blancs have toppled,
where numbers shone like heroic guard-dogs,
where the sword of syllogism flashed,
tried and tested by pure reason.
And to what end? The battle lost,
facetiousness comes into its season.

Poetry, in great distress,
furiously wrings its hands,
curses the world, feels like cutting its throat,
then laughs loudly like a maniac,
rushes outside, all of a sudden
lies down in the dust, beset by troubles.

Indeed, how did it come to pass
that the ancient capital fell at last?
The world had got used to poetry,
everything was so plausible,
the cavalry was drawn up neatly,
each gun was numbered clearly,
and Mind, blazoned on every pennant,
nodded to all, like a kindly parent.

And suddenly a bunch of elephants,
and everything turned upside down!
Poetry begins to look closely,
to study the movement of new figures,
to appreciate the beauty of awkwardness,
of the Elephant, expelled from the nether regions.

The battle is over. In the dirt
bloom the fair plants of the earth,
and the Elephant, by reason brought to heel,
eats pies and washes them down with tea!

[1931]

translated by Robin Milner-Gulland

MORNING SONG

The mighty day had come. The trees stood straight,
The foliage drew breath. And water flowed
In wooden veins. The square of window
Was opened wide above the glowing land,
And all those in the turret came together
To look upon the lustre of the sky.

And we were standing also by the window.
Dressed for the spring my wife stood there;
And young Nikita, sitting in her arms,
All bare and pink and full of laughter
In the innocuousness of purity,
Gazed at the heavens where the sun was shining.

Meanwhile on earth the trees, the beasts, the birds –
Large ones and lively, hairy ones and strong ones –
Joined in a circle; and on great guitars,
On pipes, on fiddles and on bagpipes,
Suddenly they struck up a morning song
To welcome him: and all around was singing.

And all around was singing, so that even
The billygoat went leaping round the barn.
It was that golden morning when I learnt
That there's no death and that our life's immortal.

[1932]

A GARLANDING WITH FRUIT

Michurin's fruit,[1] Burbank's cacti,[2]
translucent, like a glowing bank,
lie about in heaps and mounds –
how you trouble foolish minds!
With what translucency you shine,
when like comets, luminaries,
you lie there, forming in our midst
great Babels of lovely apples.
We engendered you, sun-fragments,
subject to the laws of human appetite,
for a new life, founded on the loftiest principles.
When, in his ignorance, a beast among the beasts,
man tyrannised the earth,
you were like crippled creatures, freaks,
suspended there in utter chaos.
The worm gnawed, and cloud-borne hail
pitted and lashed your puny frames,
while the hawk, monarch of the woods,
at night plucked out your gleaming eyes,
puckered your skin and your juices froze.

Legend has it that the Serpent chose
the apple for the depository of knowledge.
From time immemorial, the twilight world of legend,
paradise rises before us, a cloudland,
suspended among the planets, where the beasts,
with their large, blissful, cranky faces
walk, study, to chimerae offer prayers,
and talk. And towerlike, a slumbering tree
stands in the midst of heaven.
It is at the centre of the spheres,
mystery of mysteries. To right and left,
its huge boughs support a vault
of densest foliage. Sombre and severe,
through the apple-tree, God's great face peers
and floods us with its light.

. . . .

Fruit, when rivalling the clouds above
we summoned you to a better life,
when shelters were built for you,
so that the embryonic mind might flourish,
budding thought mature and grow strong,
so eyes might open on the body,
brought to perfection, so the long leaf
might learn to wield the pen, so astute bushes
might move on roots like legs, so that
from being fruit, you should become as gods,
and our existence an unbroken orchard,
tell me what wondrous gifts
will you bestow on humankind?

I should like to add you to my library,
to read you and disengage the law
conserved by you, from every angle
measure you, so as to understand the structure
of the living sun and of its incandescence.

O, heavenly bodies, sunlets, candles,
glowing in the pulp, small ovens,
warming me, warming my very eyes,
Henceforth, for me all will be translucent,
round, the earth heavy with plums,
and people in their joyful thousands
cup peaches in their hands, while barberries
demurely adorn the necks of maidens.
Here is a fort of apples, there a raspberry tower,
ponderous like shells, a pumpkin host,
and mankind, with its gigantic limbs,
sprawls, randomly conversing with the fruit.
And newly weds, who've scarce had time to kiss
gaze up at us from their apple bliss,
and we garland them, and a thousand gardens
garland us with fruit.

When Burbank lay in a chicken-coop,
investigating the fruit's first cause,
he was Adam who did not flee
the apple, so as to avoid the Fall.

He was Adam and the first gardener,
the bananas' friend, the cactus's support,
and his remains, blighted by the years,
lie now, garlanded with fruit.

[1932]

1. Ivan Vladimirovich Michurin (1845–1935), Russian horticulturist, noted for his experiments in promoting better fruit-trees by grafting.
2. Luther Burbank (1849–1926), American horticulturist. Zabolotsky became aware of him as a result of his acquaintance with the works of K.E. Tsiolkovsky, who refers to Burbank.

SIGNS OF AUTUMN

When the day is over and nature
does not chose its own illumination,
the spacious chambers of autumnal groves
hang in the air, like pristine homes.
Hawks live in them, crows pass the night,
while spectrelike the clouds above migrate.

Their pith gone, the autumn leaves
litter the ground. Far off,
a large, four-legged beast, bellowing,
strays into the misty village.
Can it be, bull, you are no longer king?
Amber now, the crowns of maple trees.

Spirit of autumn, give me the strength to write!
Diamantine is the structure of the air.
The bull has vanished from sight,
and a hazy solar sphere
glimmers above the earth,
bloodying the edges.

Revolving its eyeballs under lowered lids,
a large bird floats to the ground.
In its movement, man may be perceived.
At least, in embryo he's there.

Concealed in those great wings, he soars.
Shielded by fallen leaves a beetle cracks its door.

Architecture of autumn. In it,
the air, groves, streams,
animals and people;
ringlets flying,
leaf spirals, and a particular light –
it's these we'll chose, among the other signs.

Shielded by fallen leaves, a beetle cracks its door,
pokes out its little horns and stares.
The beetle has dug up various roots
and heaped them there.
And now it blows its tiny horn
and like a trifling god is gone.

But then the wind arrives. All that was chaste,
that was spatial, luminous, and dry,
has hardened, grown opaque, become
indistinguishable. Wind drives
the smoke, whirls the air, piles
the leaves, blows the earth sky-high.

And nature begins to freeze.
A maple leaf, coppery,
knocks against a twig.
And we must take this for a sign
sent us by nature, a token,
that we may cross into another season.

[1932]

AUTUMN

1

In a sheepskin cloak, a dog-fur crown,
the peasant stood on the river bank;
like watermarks, his cow boots shone
in the grass, his suffering face
displaying such regret,
that even the tree stooped, trembling,
and the spider ceased to spin its web.

The peasant spoke:
'Not so dear to me is the ancestral mound.
My cottage stands here like a fool,
its ancient structure now in ruins,
and cockroaches, neither black nor brown,
giant nor midget, no longer visit
the old-world portal of the oven.
And within this installation,
where, before, a pile of logs was lit,
to cook the slaughtered beast,
a little hole through to the earth has opened,
and the wind's rasping breath,
issuing from below,
shakes the cradle staves, descending
from the ceiling.
I greet you, waning luminary,
whose light carressed my cottage, who
in my ancient vegetable-garden
raised bomblike worthies, beets!
How much bright glass did you
all of a sudden light above the ox's head,
so the conjunction of its eyes
should not express primordial suffering!
Sun, farewell!
My cottage has not long to live:
beetles consume its dessicated pulp,
caterpillars break through the latrine buttresses,
and the earth worm, large and goggle-eyed,
settles on the roof and warbles like a sheik.

The peasant falls silent. He takes
from a bag a pasty stuffed with tripe,
and fills his undemanding stomach
with this wretched repast.
A crane with a pair of female breasts,
shines on a compass wheel,
and in its doleful observation of the scene,
the trees are like a cheerless dream,
stationed above the cottage roofs.
And a multitude of yellow spirals
fly in the air. Autumn's arrival
breaks the arboreal livery in two.

O, listen, listen to it clap!
In each tree perches mighty Bach,
and in each stone lurks Hannibal.
And now night comes. The forest doesn't tremble.
The river does not stir. And in the dread quiet,
with the wind passing through,
the night tree lifts
its great arms to the moon
and starts to sing. Swaying, trembling,
it sings, and with all its soul
would like to detach itself from woodenness.
But the boughs braid themselves into huge baskets,
the roots are strong, the earth is all around,
and there's no egress,
and the tree stands, weeping,
open-mouthed, and wrestling with the air.

It is no easy task to dissolve
the synonymity of nature and prison.

The peasant fell silent, and all his mental powers
simultaneously and wonderfully combined.
Thought took shape and then disintegrated,
and then again took shape. And finally,
catching himself in contemplation of a plant,
the peasant said: 'It's cause for astonishment
that the viscera of a cockroach,
laid upon the small palm of a microscope,

should excite me as much as Europe
with all its crazy confrontations.
We've got used to the multifarious conditions
of our fate, but this is not to be endured –
it makes no sense to bypass nature.'
And the peasant's trunk
suddenly takes on a beetle's traits,
rolling a last pellet of thought.
It is night, and the log walls are stout,
and the ancestors, in a heedless mass,
are grasslike, seated in the grass.

    2

The peasant enters his new kolkhoz home,
built by unprecedented labour,
that very home which is the start
of that which life, with all its strivings, promised.
The peasant walks into the common fields,
observes the placing of the grain,
listens to the earth, as it prepares to yield,
doing whatever must be done
to transform the seed, peers
into the skeleton of machines,
which stand, like children, gleaming
in the still light of the autumn stars;
his heavy eyebrows stir, as he broods.
The cow boasts of its rich blood,
the house of its heat and light,
but the machine has different affinities:
it inspires fear and uncertainty
in one who has lived a sad and lonely life
among the gifts and infirmities of nature.
The peasant walks into the vegetable garden,
where in glittering green-houses
lie fruits, protected from the birds
and the first frosts. Roundly cast,
the fruits, like little golden suns, bask,
filled with a pristine heat.
And each individual fruit's so round,
so well defined and so replete,
that, exhausted by the drawn out struggle,

the peasant senses there
a soul that suddenly lights up
with a mysterious flame. In nature,
unconcealed, so grim, malevolent, imperfect,
so sumptuous and also miserly,
there is a wonderful strength. Seize it,
inhale it, restore its parts –
and you'll be freer than a bird
among the perfected rivers and enlightened rocks.
The ancestral home, with its long shadow,
distanced itself still further from the peasant,
and a tenderness towards the living generations
drew him on forward, for many days.
The world must be different, more round,
majestic, pure, and equitable;
the world must be more intelligent, more joyful
than it was before and than it is at present.
Yes, that is true. One last time, the peasant
looks at the apples and, filling his pipe,
hurries home. Above him, like a little cube,
a chaste star glimmers in the sky,
and all is quiet. Only the sigh of leaves,
tumbling. And in the very centre of the world,
the face of Autumn, at the piano, nodding off.

[1932]

BIRDS

Scarcely fluttering,
In the contrariety of winds,
The birds, like icon-lamps,
Are suspended in the air.

Their eyes, like telescopes,
Gazed down upon the earth,
Where people crawled like bugs,
And where waters swirled.

A mouse ran across a field,
A bird dropped onto it,
And the twisted little corpse
Was borne off into the reeds.

The bird settled in the reeds.
With its toes it rent the mouse,
From its beak a liquid flowed
In a thin stream to the ground.

And drawing in the telescopes
Of its extinguished eyes,
The bird mused. A carriage
Sped along the rise.

The carriage crossed a field,
In the carriage I sat,
And my own misfortunes
Troubled me as well.

[1933]

WINTER'S START

The bright, cold start of winter
today knocked three times at my door.
I rose, went out. Metal-sharp,
the wintery air swaddled my heart.
But I breathed hard, and straightening,
ran down the hill to the level plain.
The river's fearful face stared up at me –
I shuddered as it reached into my soul.

Numbing nature with its chill, winter
trails a finger through the water.
The river trembles and, sensing its demise,
already cannot open weary eyes.
And at once its helpless body
stretches in agony, rigor sets in,

and, with leaden waters hardly stirring,
it lies now, banging its head.

For several days I watched the river as it died –
but it was only when
it threw off the cover of indifference,
that I seemed to find a way into its consciousness.
As with reason, whose frailty or strength
is fleetingly reflected in the eye,
in that little river nature showed us
its mind's own fickle world.

And I seemed to read in its lassitude
a waning tremor of thought,
and in the expression of the waves caught
sight of death. And if you know
how a man looks on the day he dies,
you'll understand the river. Already,
the water, dark as dying till half way across,
twitched with scales of ice.

And I stood beside that stone eye-socket,
seizing the last reflections of the day.
From a fir tree, huge attentive birds
stared down at me.
And then I left. Night had come.
The wind eddied, plunging into the chimney.
And the river scarcely throbbed,
as it stiffened in its stony grave.

[1935]

DROUGHT

Sun, brought to a pitch of heat,
take pity on the poor earth!
Spectres shake the atmosphere,
the golden air vibrates.
Above tattered plants,
exhalations drift, transparent beings.
How terrible, you skeletal world of flowers,
of burnt corollas, fractured leaves,
disfigured, charcoal heads,
where strays a flock of ladybirds!

In a dead faint, the river
barely moves its parched lips.
Tracing furrows in the silt,
snails crawl, poking out their horns.
Underwater wagons, carriages,
boxes of pearl and slaked lime,
enough! On this terrible day,
nothing moves before the shadows descend.
Only in the evening, when the scarlet disk
sinks behind the grove,
does the grass, weeping, come to life
and the oaks breathe,
lifting their stunted limbs.

But my life is many times more sad,
when lonely reason ails
and monstrous fantasies squat there,
lifting their snouts above the sedge.
And the soul swoons,
and doubts, like snails, creep out,
while on the sands, shivering,
blackened plants get to their feet.

And the wind and rain strike,
making the mind once more whole!
Trap the lightning in lanterns,
scoop up the crystal tones of dawn
and let the rainbow, falling on your shoulder,
colour-wash the homes of men.

Do not fear the storm! Let nature's
cleansing force strike you midships!
Even so, it will not be turned
from the path that consciousness has traced...
Teacher, virgin, mother,
you are no goddess, nor are we gods,
but still how pleasant it is to understand
your confused, chaotic lessons!

[1936]

NIGHT GARDEN

O, night garden, mysterious instrument,
forest of organ-pipes, refuge of cellos!
O, night garden, mournful procession
of mute oak-trees and motionless firs!

All day it rustled, tossing restlessly –
an uprising of poplars, a battle of oaks.
Countless leaves, like countless bodies,
flew there in unison, high or low.

Iron August, in long boots,
stood at some distance with a platter of game.
Gunfire thundered in the meadows,
birds' bodies flashed and braked.

And then the garden was silent, the moon came out,
and scores of fearful shadows lay down,
and the souls of lime-trees lifted clustered hands,
in unanimous condemnation of these crimes.

O, night garden, O poor night garden,
O beings, fallen into an endless slumber!
O you, risen over the very head
of the hazy stars, mysterious Volga!

[1936]

ALL THAT THE SOUL CONTAINED, IT SEEMED, WAS LOST AGAIN

All that the soul contained, it seemed, was lost again,
and I lay in the grass, filled with sadness and longing.
And the lovely body of a flower lifted itself above me,
and a grasshopper stood on guard before it.

And then I opened my book, in its heavy binding,
and on the very first page saw the likeness of a plant.
Lifeless, dark, either the truth of the flower
or the lie it contained, was held out to nature.

And the flower gazed in astonishment at its reflection,
and seemed to be trying to understand this alien knowledge.
Through its leaves ran a tremor of unaccustomed thought,
a flexing of the will that cannot be conveyed.

And the grasshopper lifted its trumpet, and suddenly
nature awoke, and the wistful creature sang
a gloria to the mind. And the flower's likeness
stirred in my old book, so that my heart stirred too, answering it.

[1936]

YESTERDAY, AS I THOUGHT ABOUT DEATH

Yesterday, as I thought about death,
suddenly my soul hardened.
The sadness! Ancient nature
stared at me from the darkness of the woods.
And the pain of separation was such
that in that moment everything grew audible:
the song of the grass, the water's talk,
the dull cry of a stone.
               And I drifted
above the fields, entered the forest without fear,
and dead men's thoughts, in limpid columns,
rose about me on all sides.

Pushkin's voice was heard above the foliage,
Khlebnikov's birds sang by the water's edge.[1]
A stone! The stone was motionless,
and in it Skovoroda's face appeared.[2]
And man and beast, every creature
clung to its imperishable life,
and I myself was not a child of nature,
but her thought, her inconstant mind!

[1936]

1. Velimir Khlebnikov (1885–1922), major futurist poet and visionary. Zabolotsky was greatly influenced by him.
2. Grigory Skovoroda (1722–94), Ukrainian philosopher and poet. His philosophical dialogues were imitated by Zabolotsky.

THE NORTH

In the gateway of Asia, amid dense forests,
where ancient pine-trees stand,
steeping their frigid tops in the clouds;
where the blizzard knocks the wolf off its feet;
where the stricken bird flies on
and then, with congealing blood, quivers,
dies, plunging headlong;
where in its grave-like guttering,
paved with stony ice, water,
concealed from us, barely moves
in the depths of lovely rivers;
where the sparkling air brings us
the joy of life, in its purest state,
made from crystals of cold;
where the sun's orb has a corona round it;
where people with frozen beards,
in conical, three-eared caps,
sit in sledges, and where
long columns of breath slide from their mouths;
where horses, like harnessed mammoths,
rumble; where smoke stands on the rooftops,
like a graven image to affright;

where snow sparkles as it falls upon us,
and each snow-flake, on the palm,
recalls now a little star, a ring, and now
gleams like a drumlet against the skyline,
or sinks to the ground, a tiny cross.
In the gateway of Asia, the cold's fierce embrace,
the women in fur coats, the men in sheepskins,
my native land, hiding its incalculable wealth,
lies beneath drifting snows.

And further to the north, where the polar ocean
drones on through the night, lifting the ice
perpendicularly above our heads,
where the plane, iced over,
its propeller sluggish,
descends towards these remote winter quarters –
among ice slabs, the shadow of the 'Chelyuskin',[1]
a regal spectre, looms above the gulf.

O people of the North! Blizzards of Vankarem![2]
Poem, inspired by their fortitude!
Ice that gives way under foot!
O first flight of Lyapidevsky![3]
Now, all there is orphaned:
with its billiard-ball face,
the walrus, panting, appears,
releasing into the air a spurt of steam;
shaking its shaggy mantle,
the bear passes, a hirsute demon,
in its prehistoric fur;
the sky begins to sparkle,
landscapes and buildings are revealed,
long, gleaming columns flash,
the subtlest combinations of flowers pass from the scene,
extinguished once again where chimneys rise…
The ship is invisible. Majestic ghost,
what does your glory signify?
You are imagination's breath, a phantom,
but your heroic deed bears witness –
here, in the North, the virgin icefields,
cleaving the sea's stone breast,

flotillas of huge vessels
cut an unprecedented passage through.
Like brontosauri from a fabled age,
they come, man's own creatures,
floating receptacles of wonder,
screws turning, heading into the ice.
And nature hugs them in its dead embrace,
and then, hurled back, towering in despair,
falls upon the shores
and dares not lift its head.

[1936]

1. *Chelyuskin*, a Soviet ship, which attempted the Northern sea route; on 13 February 1934, it was crushed by ice in the Chukotsk Sea.
2. Vankarem, a nomad camp of the Chukchei, where the survivors of the *Chelyuskin* were taken by plane.
3. A.V. Lyapidevskii, aviator, Hero of the Soviet Union, who first discovered the camp of the *Chelyuskin*'s survivors and took part in their rescue.

IMMORTALITY

How the world changes! And I myself!
By only one name am I known,
yet that which this name names
is not myself alone. We are many. I live.
That my blood should not freeze,
I died many times. O, how many dead bodies
have I raised from my own body!
And if only my mind could see,
with its vision penetrate the earth,
it would perceive me lying
deep among the graves! It would show me
myself, rocked on a salt-sea wave,
myself borne by the winds to unknown climes,
my wretched dust, so cherished once.

But I still live! More resolutely,
a world filled with magic creatures
enfolds the spirit. Nature is alive. Live

in the fields, both the living grain and my dead herbarium.
Thing into thing, form into form. The world,
in all its living architecture,
is a full-throated organ, a piano, an ocean of horns,
well supplied, whether in joy or storm.
How all changes! What was a bird before
now lies here, like a page of words,
a thought was once a simple flower,
a poem moves to the solemn measure of an ox,
and that which was myself
may rise again, increasing the world of plants.

And so, trying hard to unravel
what seems to be a tangled web,
suddenly you see what one can only call
immortality. O,
to what superstitions we are prey!

[1937]

Post-imprisonment Poems

A WOODLAND LAKE

Again the flash of that dream-held cup,
Crystalline, caught my eye in the dark.

Past struggling trees and battling wolves,
Where suckling insects sip on plants,
Where stalks run riot and flowers moan,
Where predatory nature rules its creation,
I broke through to you and on the threshold
Fell silent, as I parted the undergrowth.

Girdled with lilies, in a head-dress of sedge,
A brittle chaplet of vegetal pipes,
Lay this undefiled patch of liquidity,
A shelter for ducks, an asylum for fish.
And yet how strangely solemn it was!
How did such grandeur possess these brakes?
Why, instead of going berserk,
Do the bird hosts slumber, lulled by dreams?
A solitary sandpiper regrets his lot,
Foolish notes fluted abroad.

And the lake, in the smouldering of evening,
Shines on, motionless in its depth,
While about it the tapering pines, in their height,
Close up ranks from end to end.
The bottomless chalice of limpid water
Glows, preoccupied with its thoughts...

So, a dying man, with infinite longing,
At the first flash of the evening star,
Unconscious now of his ailing body,
Turns burning eyes to the night sky.
And the hordes of animal creatures, thrusting
Horned faces between the firs,
At this font of truth, their very own,
Drink of the life-sustaining waters.

[1938]

THE NIGHTINGALE

The woodland choir had fallen silent,
The siskin had scarcely opened its throat,
In a leafy crown, the nightingale
Rings out endlessly over the world.

The more I rebuffed you, perfidious passions,
The less was I able to laugh in your face.
Is it in your power, diminutive creature,
To hold your tongue in this temple of light?

Slant rays, falling upon the chill surface
Of leaves, whirled away into space.
The more I put loyalty to the test,
The less I believed in its permanence.

And you, nightingale, captive of art,
Antony in love with his Cleopatra,
How could you, madcap, trust in feeling,
How be transported by love's pursuit?

And why, abandoning the groves of evening,
Do you break my heart into tiny morsels.
I am ill with you, and it would be easier
To part now and distance myself from misfortune.

Already the world seems made so the creatures
That begot the first, stark symphonies,
Hearing your exclamations, should bellow
And howl their 'Antony! Antony!'

[1939]

Note: 'A Woodland Lake' seems to have been composed during Zabolotsky's train journey to the labour camps in the Far East and written down after his realease. 'The Nightingale' was composed in spring, in the camp near Komsomolsk, on the Amur, and was written down after the poet was released in 1944, in the Altai Region of the Far East. It is the only poem he composed in the camps.

THE BLIND MAN

Face turned to the sky,
Head uncovered,
He looms at the gate,
This god-cursed old man.
All day he sings,
And his sad, angry chant
Strikes to the core,
And startles the passers-by.

And around the old man,
The young ones clamour.
Blossoming,
The crazed lilac moans.
And in the cherry-tree grotto,
Through the silvery foliage,
The dazzling day
Climbs into the sky.

Blindman, why do you weep,
Why do you long for spring?
Of your earlier hopes,
Not a trace remains.
Your dark abyss,
The burgeoning shall not cover,
Your nearly dead eyes,
You'll not open again.

And your entire life
Is one great wound.
Out of favour of the sun,
No kinsman of nature either,
You have learnt to live
In eternal fog,
You have learnt to look
Into the face of darkness...

And I tremble to think
That somewhere, on the edge of nature,
I am just such a blindman,

My face turned to the sky.
Only in the darkness of my soul
Do I gaze on the vernal waters,
Converse with them
Only in my sorrowing heart.

How hard it is
To look at earthly objects.
Wrapped in the fog of habit,
I am heedless, bitter, vain!
These songs of mine,
How often has the world heard them!
Where shall I still find words
For the sublime song of life.

And where are you leading me,
Dark, terrible muse,
Over what great highways
Of this boundless land?
Never, never
Did I ask to be one with you,
Nor ever wish
To submit to your will –

It was you who chose me,
Who got into my soul,
Opened my eyes
To the wonders of the earth...
So, sing, blind old man!
Night draws near. Far off,
The planets, echoing you,
Shine impassively.

[1946]

THUNDERSTORM

The tormented summer lightning shudders, as it courses above
    the earth,
Cloud shadows lie down, merge, blend with the grass.
It grows harder to breathe, in the sky the cloud bank stirs,
A bird drifts by, passing low above my head.

I love this rapturous half-light, this brief night of inspiration,
The human rustle of the grass, on the hand a prophetic chill,
This lightning-flash of thought, this deliberation
Of distant thunder, first words in their own tongue.

So, from the dark water, a bright-eyed maiden rises,
And the waters flow over her body and freeze in ecstasy.
The grasses swoon, and to left and to right
The flocks divide at the sight of this sky.

And over the water, over the wide circle of the earth,
Astounded, she gazes, in her naked effulgence.
And sporting with the thunder, the word rolls in a white cloud,
And gleaming rain explodes on the happy flowers.

[1946]

BEETHOVEN

That very day when your accords
Surmounted the complex world of labour,
Light subdued light, cloud traversed cloud,
Thunder browbeat thunder, star entered star.

And in a frenzy of inspiration,
Amid orchestral storms, shudder of thunderclaps,
You climbed the nebulous stairway
And grazed the music of the spheres.

With your trumpet-grove, your lake of melody,
You overcame the dissonance of the storm,

And in the very face of nature shouted,
Your lion's head thrust between organ pipes.

And in the presence of terrestrial space,
You invested this shout with such significance
That speech, with a howl, tore itself from speech
And became music, haloing your lion's face.

Again the lyre sounded in the bull's horns,
The eagle's bone a shepherd's flute,
And you understood the living magic of the world,
And separated its evil from its good.

And through the tranquility of space,
The ninth wave rolled, reaching the very stars ...
Thought, be manifest! Speech, be as music,
Strike to the core, that the world might rejoice!

[1946]

translated by Peter Levi and Robin Milner-Gulland

O TREES, RECITE HESIODIC HEXAMETERS

O, trees, recite Hesiodic hexameters,
be amazed by Ossian, mountain ash;
nature, it is not your long sword that sounds
against the shield of Cuchulain but the school-bell's crash.
The wind is neverending like an epic poet.
The birch forest of Morven is still crying out Irish,
but look, in the schoolhouse hares and sparrows sit:
now the ninth muse has descended to the animal.
Birches you are schoolgirls, you are chattering, be quiet,
stop that horseplay and tearing your skirts and all.
Through the storm and the mud listen how the waterfalls roar;
they have joined their tongues and where the willow branches
      fall
into that mirror of rivers and fir trees paw the air
the small Hamlet voice of the grasshopper is groaning.

To put an end to uncertainties you must be stronger.
and again I recognize that nature is deceiving,
nature is an old madam with a house full of whores;
Why, why am I in this dirt and downpour, why am I wandering
like a mad creature? how many times and with what force
nature said there can be no immortal illusions of the intellect
at the moment of general decay: life's a moment or worse.
I disbelieved nature and I cannot now expect
another miracle than this one I am singing about in my heart
before my soul shakes loose and my body is derelict.
Look, we have been the masters of this world from the start:
we are the sages and the pedagogues of the universe;
I hear through woods and brakes the loud harp-strings of
    Ossian's art,
from one sea to the other we can teach, we breed our brothers,
and each day playing slowly in sunlight some butterflies
settle to rest on the balding head of Socrates.

[1946]

translated by Peter Levi and Robin Milner-Gulland

IN THIS BIRCH WOOD

Oriole sing an empty song
in this birch wood
far from trouble,
where the pink stare of daybreak trembles
and the transparent avalanches
of leaves cascade from high branches:
the song of my life.

Fly over us, spy glade out
take a too tiny to be seen
wooden flute
and visit my morning –
in the fresh hours of the morning –
and at my human door
sing matins virtuous and poor.

But still we are soldiers and men;
and an atomic explosion
flings up houses, a white whirlwind
on the boundary of mind
the war flaps its banners round
like a mad windmill in the wind.
Why are you silent my friend?
Hermit in the forest, O bird.

Flying through bombardment
where black rushes line the stream
and high over ravines
or death and his ruins
silently wandering
into battle my friend
there is a fatal cloud
low and loud
over your head.

The sun will rise beyond the great rivers,
sunken-templed I shall drop with the killed
in the morning's dark moment.
Machine-guns cry out like the wild
raven, shake and grow quiet;
in my torn heart
your note will start.

Above the birch wood
above my birches
where rosy avalanches
of leaves drop from high branches,
where the fragments of a flower
grow cold under the rainshower
century beyond century
will solemnize eternal victory.

[1946]

I TOUCHED THE LEAVES OF THE EUCALYPTUS

I touched the leaves of the eucalyptus
And the firm plumes of the agave,
Their evening chorus chanting,
Adzharia's succulent grasses.
In white dress the magnolia
Inclined its hazy form,
And the blue sea of Georgia
Sang intemperately by the shore.

But in the glare of nature,
I dreamt of my Moscow woods,
Where the sky, the sky is paler,
The plants are more humble and plain,
Where the gentle oriole moans
Above a glowing vision of the meadow,
And where my companion
Gazes, full of sorrow.

And the pain of it made me shudder,
And tears of sadness fell
Onto the chalices
Of plants where white birds call.
And against the sky, the laurels,
Aromatic, grey with dust,
Blew their pallid bugles,
Sounded their kettledrums.

[1947]

LODEINIKOV[1]

1

In a land of wonders, of living plants,
infused with a wisdom still imperfect,
why do you hunger after new experiences
and new disturbances, inquisitive spirit?
Do not be seduced by the illusion of peace,
the eye is too easily deceived.
The hour will come and that fatal morning
will dazzle you and disperse your dreams.

2

Lodeinikov, covering his face with his hands,
lay in the garden. Evening had arrived.
Below, the delicate cowbells tinkled,
as the herd made its way home, mumbling
its inarticulate memories.
The cold breath of the grass
took to the road, a beetle to the air.
Lodeinikov uncovered his face and gazed
at the grass. It lifted before him,
in a wall of vessels. And each vessel
fleshy, gleamed with veins. And all this flesh
trembled, grew tall, while a drone
spread through the earth. With a cracking of joints,
shuffling, moving in a strange manner,
the vast forest of grass stretched to the right,
where the setting sun still glowed.
And then there was a battle of grass, a mute battle of plants.
Some, drawing themselves up into lush funnels,
shedding their leaves, trampled others down,
and their strained articulations secreted
a thick mucus. Some crawled into cracks
between the leaves, while others
lay heavily on their neighbours
and pulled them back, wearing them out.

And at this moment the beetle blew upon his pipe.
Lodeinikov woke. Over the village
rose the moon's misty crescent,

and gradually the murmur of grass
and of the stillness turned to song.
Nature sang. The forest, lifting its face,
sang along with the meadow. The stream,
rang out in bell-like clarity.
In the white mist,
grasshoppers shook their brittle pads,
black armfuls of beetles stood by,
their voices twiglike.
Handsome Sokolov crossed the meadow,
his spectacles glittering,
and pensively strummed his guitar.
The flowers brushed against his boots
and bowed down. Small creatures
hurtled into his chest,
dropping to the ground.
With indifference Sokolov trod this offal,
continuing on his way.

Lodeinikov began to weep. Around him,
fireflies lit their lamps,
but his mind, alas, for no good reason,
with itself was playing hide-and-seek.

    3
In his little cabin, seated at the table,
sorrowing, he pondered.
Already dusk had gathered. All around
nocturnal birds called plaintively.
A flickering light spilled through the windows,
and in its uncertain radiance
apple trees stood like statues
that had descended from antiquity.
A flickering light passed through the windows,
so each little petal,
like a transparent cup, open to the east,
was etched in the hazy foliage,
and the wonderful and precious plant
reminded each of us
of a perfect work of nature,
made for perfected eyes to gaze upon.

Lodeinikov bent over sheets of paper,
and at that moment there appeared
a huge worm. Seizing a sheet between iron teeth,
it drew back into the gloom.
So, this is nature's celebrated harmony,
these are the voices of the night!
So this is what the waters babble in the dark,
what the sighing forests whisper!
Lodeinikov listened. Over the garden
passed the murmur of a thousand deaths.
Nature casually went about its hellish business.
The beetle ate the grass, the bird spiked the beetle,
the ferret sucked the bird's brains from its head,
and the fear-distorted faces of the night's creatures
peered up from the grass.
Nature's everlasting wine-press
mingled life and death,
but thought was powerless
to join its own two mysteries.

And the moonlight flowed from around the cornice.
In her plain bonnet, Larisa the thrifty heiress,
her ashen cheeks rouged,
stepped onto the porch.
Lodeinikov was not for her.
She wanted singing, dancing, merry-making,
whereas he was morose and dull. Across the river
a motley band of maidens cavorted.
There Sokolov strutted with his guitar.
To him, to him! He serenaded them,
mocked and taunted every pair
and godlike kissed each lovely thing.

4

Stern autumn's tardy face is sad.
Downcast, the voiceless plants are sleeping.
Over the roofs of the deserted village,
a cloudy sunset faintly glows.
The doors of the little huts are shut,
the gardens have emptied, the fields are lifeless,
the frozen ground about the tossing trees

is littered with glittering curls,
the sky glowers, and the wind
blows stiffly in our face,
bending in two the canopied trees.

O, listen, listen to the applause!
In each tree mighty Bach is seated,
Hannibal lurks in every stone…
And now Loedeinikov can't sleep at night.
In the orchestral storms, he hears
the forests' wistful, passionate note.
At the station, one rainy day,
he bade young Larisa farewell.

How poor Larisa has changed!
All that had graced her youth,
on some strange impulse she
had surrendered to a casual acquaintance.
The traces of her tears had still not dried
in Sokolov's cold heart.
The autumn wind carried off
all that had once been.
Ah, Lara, foolish Lara,
who could help you?
Through your life passed his guitar
and a voice, slow like the night.
The oaks that night rustled so pleasantly,
the lilac bloomed, the cherry blossomed,
and the nocturnal songsters serenaded you,
as though you were, indeed, a bride,
as though, indeed, this sparkling garden
were covered with a silvery bridal veil…
And only the bittern, sobbing, called
beyond the river, until dawn.

From his silent carriage,
huddling there, like a feeble old man,
for the last time Lodeinikov
gazed sadly and lovingly at her dear face.
And the train pulled out. But the voices of the plants
carried after, swaying, trembling,

and through the deep, conciliatory night,
the vegetable world's immortal soul
rushed on. Hour after hour,
time raced by. And in the fields
a huge city instantly sprang up,
blazing with myriad lights.
The elements of the unco-ordinated world
now merged in a single choir,
as if to try out the forest instruments.
A new conductor had entered upon nature.
To the organ cliffs he lent the appearance of pit-faces,
to the river orchestras, the iron pace of turbines,
and turning the plunderer from his preying ways
he exulted, like a wise old giant.
And already the first harmonious notes
mingled with nature's dissonant voices,
as if the waters suddenly sensed
that their grave malady was not fatal,
as if the grasses suddenly sensed
that there was a sun of everlasting days,
that, in the universe, it was not they
who were the righteous ones,
but only he, the great enchanter.

Stern autumn's tardy face is sad,
but your star, nature,
burns in the night,
and with it burns my soul.

[1932–1947]

1. The prototype for Lodeinikov is, perhaps, N. M. Oleinikov (1898–1937), children's writer, parodist and associate of Zabolotsky and Kharms in the OBERIU group. He was arrested and shot early during the purges. This is a composite poem, based on two earlier poems: 'Lodeinikov' and 'Lodeinikov in the Garden'. In 1947, Zabolotsky had intended to write a cycle, with Lodenikov as its hero, using the two earlier fragments, plus new material. The project was never realized and only fragments of this larger design, translated here, remain.

Translator's note: I have translated 'Lodeinikov' into free-verse, as with a number of other mid-length poems (e.g. 'A Garlanding with Fruit'), since I was more able to preserve the visionary descriptiveness by so doing. There is considerably more enjambment in 'Lodeinikov' than is usual with Zabolotsky.

translated by Peter Levi and Robin Milner-Gulland

I DO NOT LOOK FOR HARMONY IN NATURE

I do not look for harmony in nature
I do not discern in the inward parts of rocks
I do not discern in the clear roof of leaves
any proportionable origins.

It is a world of sleep and unreason.
The heart hears no concordant music
in the obstinate chanting of the wind,
the soul senses neither voice nor harmony.

When in the silence of the sunsets of autumn
the wind dies in the remote distance,
when night comes down blindly to the river
all interfused with puny radiance,
and when the black water weary of its vigour
its bodily movement and its massive labours
drops into the disturbed half-sleep of exhaustion,
and is silent,
when the huge world of contradictions halts
a kind of archetype of human pain
rises to me from the abyss of waters.

Around me nature's sad and heavy breathing.
And wild freedom and good mixed with evil
are not in nature at this moment.

It is a dream of glittering turbines,
measured voices of labour and reason,
the chanting pipes the pink glow of the dam,
electric power, human construction.

Lovesick, brainless mother: slack on her bed
with her child's whole world hidden in her
will wake into daylight with her son.

[1947]

TESTAMENT

When the years tilt and my life drains away,
when I blow out the candle and set off
into the unmeasured universe of mist and metamorphosis,
when million on million generations
fill this whole world with miracles of light,
when they complete this half-constructed work that nature is,
let my ashes be in these waters,
let me be in this wood.

O friend, I will not die but be made known
to this world in the musk breath of flowers,
and many-centuried the oak will knot my soul alive
into its root, sadly and austerely;
I will be the mind's shelter in its leaves,
and in those big branches my own thoughts be cherished and live,
above you in the dark wood
a common consciousness.

And I shall be a slow bird through the sky
above your head, distant descendant,
the pale sheet-lightning bursting above you,
the pouring rain of summers glistening in grass.
There is no light as bright as existence.
The wordless grave is an empty languor.
I have lived out my life and not seen peace.
There is no peace.
My presence. Life's presence.

I was not born when I looked first
from the cradle to the world,
I thought first when the hard crystal sensed,
because the raindrop fell on it,
disintegrating rays of light.

I have not lived on earth without meaning,
and it is sweet to strive out of darkness
for you to hold me distant descendant

on the palm of your hand and to finish
what I did not finish.

[1947]

CRANES

Leaving Africa, in April,
For the shores of their own land,
In a long v-formation,
The cranes melted into the sky.

Flexing silvery wings,
Over the expanse of the heavens,
The leader led his little band
Towards the valley of abundance.

But when the lake beneath them shone,
Transparent through and through,
Out of the bushes, a black muzzle
Rose to greet them.

A fiery ray struck to the bird's heart,
The brief flame flared and went out,
And a fragment of sheer grandeur
Dropped onto us from above.

Two huge wings, like sorrow twinned,
Embraced the stony waters,
And the cranes with reiterated sobbing,
Streamed away into the heights.

Only there, where planets move,
Atoning for the evil done,
Did nature once again return
What death had taken away:

The proud spirit, high aspirations,
A warrior's unbending will,
All that is handed down to youth
From the earlier generation.

And the leader, in his steely coat,
Sank slowly to the bottom,
While above him dawn brushed in
A glowing patch of gold.

[1948]

LATE SPRING

The late spring sun, as it rises
ever higher into the sky,
lights the tiles of the rooftops
and warms the tapering pines.

In the rosy haze of branches,
budding but leafless still,
with sunlight slanting between them,
the nightingale flutters and sings.

How natural it sounds,
this laconic rehearsal of themes,
as if the diminutive creature
were singing just for you and me!

O deception dear to the heart,
delusion precious to youth!
On that day when the glades turn green,
there is no escaping you.

Like Copernicus, I disrupted
the spheres' Pythagorean song,
and revealed what lay at its root –
just the prattle, the music of wings.

[1948]

TOWARDS THE MIDDLE OF APRIL

It was towards the middle of April; the stream tumbled down
the slope; day and night, on the weir, the wooden spillway
thundered.

Under bedraggled willow trees, each one a poor, crippled thing,
that day I noticed a man I had not seen before.

He stood and held out in front of him an unbroken loaf of bread,
and with his free hand he leafed through the pages of an old book.

Care had furrowed his brow, and plainly he was not robust, but
also he could not cease from intellectual toil.

Running through page after page, he raised his eyes and,
marvelled, staring at the streams that converged, in sequence, on
the foaming race.

And at that moment, what had been hidden from him before was
revealed, and his soul rose into the world, like a child rising from
its crib.

But the rooks called with such frenzy, and the willows' din was
so fierce, that it seemed they would not allow the last vestige of
sorrow to be lifted from him.

[1948]

In Zabolotsky's short autobiographical piece 'Early Years', he describes a notice over
his father's library to the effect that books were as important as bread. When the family
lived in Peredelkino, after Nikolay Zabolotsky's return from the camps, the poet would
sometimes take a break from his work and have a drink with friends in a café by the lake
where the wooden spillway was situated. It was on one such occasion that he saw the
man, with the round loaf in one hand and a book in the other.

Translator's note: I have translated this poem (rhyming quatrains) into prose, while
keeping the stanzaic divisions. My excuse for so doing is that the translation was prosaic
anyway and that attempts to imitate the form only blurred or distorted the narrative.

FIRE-FLIES

Words are like fire-flies with lanterns.
If you are lost and haven't searched the dusk,
Their virginal flame seems darkly insignificant,
And imperceptible their animated dust.

But in the South, in springtime Sochi,
Where festive, blooming oleanders sleep,
A sea of fire-flies glows in the gulf of night,
And winged waves, sobbing, on the sea-shore beat.

The whole world fused in a single breath,
From underneath your feet, the round globe slips away.
And already it is not their light affirms the universe,
But the distant thunder's intermittent blaze.

The breath of unfamiliar bells, of bugles,
Drones on, feeling out the heights.
What are words? Pitiful! Like insects!
And yet these creatures heard me and obeyed.

[1949]

Nikita Zabolotsky remembers the occasion when the whole family was walking along a bluff, the sea below, in Sochi, RSFSR. They saw the fire-flies. There was distant thunder. His father stopped for a moment and stared out to sea. When they got home, he wrote this poem.

MEMORY

The months of drowsiness are upon us...
Either life has truly passed,
Or like a belated guest, its work all done,
It is sitting down with us at last.

It wants to drink, but no wines please,
To eat, it cannot swallow.
It listens to the whispering rowan trees,
The goldfinch just outside the window.

The bird is singing of that distant country,
Where, through a driving storm, the mound
Of a solitary grave is scarcely noticed
In the crystal whiteness all around.

Its creeping root-stock in the icy crust,
The whispering birch tree does not answer.
Encircled by a filmy hoop of frost,
Above, the blood-stained moon meanders.

[1952]

translated by Peter Levi and Robin Milner-Gulland

GOODBYE TO FRIENDS

In broadbrimmed hats and long overcoats
        with whole notebooks full of your poems
long, long ago you crumbled to ashes,
        like leafless lilac branches.

In that country no shape is ready-made
        all is mingled, dislocated, broken,
        and the only sky is the heap of the grave
        and the moon's orbit does not move.

And the noiseless insect assembly sings
  in another and indistinct language,
  and the man-beetle welcomes his friends
  with a small lantern in his hand.

  Is it peaceful for you, old comrades?
Are you easy? Do you forget everything?
   How your brothers are ants and grasses
and roots and heaps of dust and sighs.

Your sisters are the pinks and lilac nipples,
the chickens in the woodshavings, you cannot
remember the language of your brother,
who has no place yet in the country where

light you disappeared like shadows
in broadbrimmed hats and long overcoats
with whole notebooks full of your poems.

[1952]

Note: written in memory of D. Kherms and A. Vredensky, ten years after their deaths.

DREAM

Earth-dweller, fifty years of age,
Like everybody, both happy and unhappy,
One day I left this world of ours,
Finding myself, then, in a silent country.
There man's existence was in doubt,
The last vestiges of habit clinging,
Anonymous, answering to no name,
He did not hanker after anything.
And drawn into this singular game,
With no eye for the clustered faces,
I lay down among smouldering fires,
Rose and lay down again ad infinitum.
But then I floated off. I travelled far,
Weak-willed, indifferent, taciturn,
And with a lazy gesture brushed aside

The vanished world's faint reflection.
Within me, an echo of
My earlier existence lingered,
But already my entire spirit strove
To be, instead, joined to the universe.
Towards me, through space, came
A combination of material objects,
Bridges of inestimable height
Were suspended over vast abysses.
I well remembered how these things once looked,
All these bodies that came towards me, floating:
Network of girders, bulkiness of slabs,
And the artlessness of primal decoration.
Of subtlety not a trace remained,
Nor, it seems, was form held in high regard,
And it was clear that toil made no claim,
Although this world moved, and all worked hard.
And in the conduct of the powers that be,
Force was not discernible,
And I myself, desireless, deprived of will,
Did what must be done, without exertion.
I had no reason not to wish, just as
There was no wish to strive for anything,
And I was prepared to journey on,
If doing so might serve some greater purpose.
I was companioned by a little child.
He chattered to me, babbling on and on,
And even he, although much like
A wraith, was more material than of the spirit.
This child and I walked towards a lake,
He cast a line that drifted downwards,
And something wafting up to us from earth
He brushed aside with a casual gesture…

[1953]

PORTRAIT

Poets, cherish painting!
For only art can capture
The fickle soul, its traces,
And set them down on canvas.

Do you recall how Struiskaya,[1]
Wrapped in a satin whispiness,
Gazed out once more at us
From Rokotov's portrait?[2]

A mist swims in her eyes,
Half smiling, half in tears,
Her gaze dissembling, dark
With consciousness of defeat.

In these eyes is an enigma,
Part rapture, part dread,
And an impulse to tenderness,
Anticipation of the end.

When the darkness presses,
And the thunderstorm draws near,
Deep within I catch the glimmer
Of this lady's lovely eyes.

[1953]

1. A.P. Struiskaya's misty and enigmatic portrait hangs in the Tretyakov Gallery, Moscow.
2. Fyodor Stepanovich Rokotov (1730–1808) was a celebrated portrait painter of the period.

translated by Robin Milner-Gulland

POET

Black is the pine-wood behind this old house:
In front of it, a field with growing oats.
A cloud of unimagined beauty
Hangs in the soft sky like a ball of silver.
Mistily lilac-hued to either side
But in the middle bright and menacing –
The wing of a wounded swan
Drifting slowly away.
While below, upon the old veranda
There stands a grey-haired youth:
Like a portrait in an antique circlet
Made of field camomile-flowers,
He peers through slant-cut eyes,
Warmed by the sun of the Moscow countryside –
Forged and hammered in the storms of Russia:
Poet, and my heart's interlocutor.
And all the while the forests stand like night
Behind the house: in front, the oats thrust crazily...
That which before was alien to the heart
Is here made close to it.

[1953]

The poet is Boris Pasternak, the place his dacha in Peredelkino.

RETURNING FROM WORK

Thunder prowled the village.
Through the weeping,
Tormented flashes struck at
The sky, shattering it.

And the heavens emptied themselves,
And above the birch-trees,
There was a chaotic, frenzied mingling
Of electricity and moisture!

And we marched along the road,
Grasslands stretching either side,
Like gods of ancient Greece,
Tridents jabbing at the clouds.

[1954]

FLIGHT INTO EGYPT

Guardian of my days, an angel
With a lamp sat in the room,
Keeping watch over the dwelling
Where I lay on my sick bed.

By disease debilitated,
Distanced from my friends,
I slumbered on. One after another
Visions passed before my eyes.

And I dreamt I was an infant,
Wrapped in finest swaddling clothes,
Brought to this distant country
By a settler from Judea.

Before the tyrant Herod's ruffians
We had trembled. And yet now,
In this white house, with its veranda,
We'd found a refuge for ourselves.

By the olive-tree, the donkey
grazed. I tumbled in the sand.
Further off, mother and Joseph
Pottered happily about.

Often in the Sphynx's shadow,
I would rest, and the bright Nile,
Like a lens, brimming over,
Mirrored the planets above.

And in this misty luminescence,
Lit by the irridescent flames,
Spirits, angels, children played me
Pleasant tunes upon their pipes.

But when it came to us, the notion
Of returning to our home,
And Judea unfolded
The dreaded image of itself –

Poverty, wretchedness,
Servility, intolerance, fear,
Where the crucified one's shadow
Lay across the slums,

I cried out and awoke in horror…
By the lamp, next to the fire,
In angelic luminescence,
Your gaze shone full on me.

[1955]

In a field, somewhere near Magadan,
Danger and disaster all about,
In the mist's freezing exhalations,
They trailed behind the sledge.
From the iron palate of the soldiers,
From the brigand bands that preyed on them,
Only the aid-post could protect them now,
And details into town to fetch some meal.
Two old men, in pea-jackets,
Two unfortunates, far from home,
Remembering their distant villages
And yearning for them, on they walked,
Far from their dear ones, from family,
They were used up, all passion spent,
And the weariness that bowed their bodies,
Tonight consumed their souls as well.
Life, in the forms decreed by nature,
Ran its course above their heads.
But the stars, signifying freedom,
Turned their faces from the ways of men.
The universe's wonder play was staged
In the luminous theatre of the North,
Yet its intense and penetrating flame
No longer reached into the human heart.
The blizzard moaned and whistled,
Burying the frigid stumps of trees,
On which, not looking at each other,
Silently the two old Russians sat.
The horses stood, the work was over,
All mortal affairs were ended now...
And a drowsiness held them sweetly captive,
And sobbing led them into distant parts.
No more will the guard herd them together,
Nor will the escort rope them in.
Only the lovely constellations
Of Magadan will sparkle overhead.

[1956]

from LAST LOVE

1 *Thistle*

A bunch of thistles was brought in,
Set on the table, and at once
Fire broke out, there was confusion,
A crimson round-dance of flames.
These stars, bristling with spikes,
These splashes, shards of a northern dawn,
Jingled and moaned like little bells,
Blazing like lamps from within.
This, too, is an image of the universe,
An organism woven out of rays,
The flashing of an undecided battle,
The glitter of uplifted blades.
Here is a tower of fury and of honour,
Where spear contends with spear,
Where bunches of flowers, bloody-headed,
Are etched onto my heart.
I dreamt of a high prison cell,
Its bars, black as night,
And behind these bars the fabled bird,
She whom no person could help.
But plainly I, too, do not lived as I should,
Since neither have I the strength to help her.
And the wall of thistles lifts itself
Between me and my happiness.
And a wedge-shaped thorn has stabbed my breast,
And already, for a last time,
Her inextinguishable eyes
Turn their sad, glowing gaze on me.

[1956]

2 *Sea Excursion*

In the gleaming, white speed-boat,
We entered the stone grotto,
And the capsized body of the rock
Screened us from the curious heavens.
In this glimmering, subterranean chamber,
Above the transparent lagoon,

We ourselves became translucent,
Like mica figurines.
And in the great crystal bowl
Our dim reflections gazed
Back up at us, in amazement,
With a million glittering eyes –
As though shoals of fish-tailed maidens
And scuttling, crablike boys,
Breaking loose from the gulf,
Had thrown a cordon round our boat.
Under the sea's vast cover,
An entire world of sorrow and rejoicing
Mimed the movements of men,
Living out its prodigious life.
Something seethed; it burst,
Then fused, then burst again,
And the flesh of the overturned rock,
Above us, was breached right through.
But the skipper pressed down on the pedal,
And again, as in a dream,
We flew from this world of sadness,
Buoyed high on a surging wave.
Our stern was running with foam,
The sun, at its zenith, flamed,
And Taurida rose from the sea,
Drawing closer to your face.

[1956]

4 *Last Love*
The car shuddered and stopped,
Two descended into the evening,
And the exhausted driver yawned
And slumped over the wheel.

Far off, through the windows,
Fiery constellations flickered.
The elderly passenger lingered
With his friend by the flower-bed.

There were flame-headed cannae there,
Like beakers of blood-red wine,

Golden-wreathed camomile,
And the grey plumes of columbine.

And mutely leaning together,
Homeless children of the night,
Silently they circled the flowers,
In the electric glare of the lights.

But the car stood in the darkness,
Its motor's insistently throbbing,
And the driver wound down the window,
Smiling wearily in his cab.

[1957]

Translator's note: I have taken it upon myself to delete three passages, in which, for instance, the driver's thoughts, as he watches the two lovers, are described. In resorting to this drastic procedure (the only time I have done so) I was trying to avoid the descent into bathos, which – try as I might – affected my English version of the whole. The poem, not divided into stanzas in the original, divides naturally, it seems to me, into four quatrains here.

8   *The Juniper Bush*

In my dreams I saw a juniper bush,
I heard, far off, its metallic crunch,
The ring of its amethyst berries I heard,
And in my dream, in the stillness, was glad.

I sensed through my dream the faint resinous smell,
And pushing aside the low juniper stems,
In the woodland darkness I then caught sight
Of the glimmering likeness of your smile.

Juniper bush, juniper bush,
Chatter, prattle of volatile lips
That stiffen, the resinous smell nearly gone,
Pricking me with its lethal thorn!

Through my window, above, in the golden skies,
One after another, the clouds float by,
My garden stripped bare, comes a lifeless hush...
May god forgive you, juniper bush!

[1957]

9 The Meeting

> And the face, with its watchful eyes, smiled with difficulty, with an effort,
> like a rusted door opening... (Tolstoy, *War and Peace*)

Like a creaky door that must be forced,
she, my unexpected visitor,
forgetting what had been,
opened her face when she saw me.
And light streamed out – or rather, a vibrant
sheaf of rays – and not just that,
a superabundance of spring, of joy.
And ever the misanthropist,
I was confused... And in this exchange of ours,
in our smiles, our exclamations –
yet not so much in them, as behind, beyond them –
an inextinguishable light now shone
that took possession of my mind.
We opened the window and looked out at the garden,
and innumerable moths senselessly cascaded,
in a weightless, multicoloured stream,
over the brilliant lampshade.
One of them settled on my shoulder,
transparent, palpitating, pinkly luminescent.
I had no questions yet to ask...
Besides, there was no need of them – of questions.

[1957]

FOREST-LODGE

It creaked, and whistled, and howled in the forest,
The distant thunder was like hammer blows,
And clouds erupted, while below,
Silence, and dusk, and coldness reigned.
In the gigantic well of conifer trunks,
In his lonely, wretched lodge,
The keeper ate, unsmiling, silent,
Brushing the crumbs of bread onto his palm.
Above the world, a great storm gathered,
But here, in the quiet, by the stubborn roots,
The old man rested and gave it no thought,
And only the dog growled despondently
At each far-off flash of summer-lightning,
While the bird-village fell silent in the trees.

Once, in such a storm, there came to his home
A shaggy creature that loomed at the door,
And just as any other might have done,
When it saw the man, startled, it fled.
And the keeper seized his old Berdan gun,
The cat sprang from the sill and hid under the stairs,
And suddenly a shot rang out,
Shaking the forest to its foundations.

Returning, the keeper soon regained his calm,
He had lived long enough to know
That peace is only a semblance of itself,
That when the storm flashes and growls,
All that's most wickedly alive, most feral,
Rises to look man in the eye.

[1957]

POULTRY YARD

The many-sided poultry yard
Hops, mutters, peeps.
A mighty rooster yells,
A turkey chorus shrieks.

And in this extravagant din,
Amid the twittering of chicks,
Geese grandiosely churn
The mud with stubby kicks.

And teetering from side to side,
Obliquely across the pound,
Ducks firmly plant
Their webbed prints on the ground.

If I were a bird, like these,
Vibrant, ablaze with life,
I'd take to the skies in haste,
Slip out from beneath the knife!

But they've no faith in miracles.
All they think about is food,
And so they wait mindlessly, until
They take leave of their heads.

Endless din, eternal trampling.
Endlessly foolish, pompous air,
Experience of life, it's clear,
Has taught them nothing.

Their hearts obediently beat,
By courtesy of humankind.
And in them the free swans'
Yearning cries do not resound.

[1957]

translated by Robin Milner-Gulland

LONG AGO

Long ago
A man bitter and wasted from hunger
Walked through a graveyard,
Was just going through its gate –
When beside a fresh cross
On a muddy, low grave
An unremarked person
Noticed and called to him.

An old country woman –
Shawl threadbare, hair grey,
Silent, sad, stooping –
Lifted herself off the ground,
And with her dark claw of a hand
Crossed herself, proferred him
One little egg
And two wafers for ritual remembrance.

Then lightning flashed in his heart:
And in the same instant
Hundreds of trumpets cried out,
The skies scattered stars on him.
Wretched and crushed,
In the glow of those suffering eyes
He accepted the gift
And partook of the bread of remembrance.

It was all long ago.
And now, as a poet of standing –
Though by no means much liked
Nor, for that matter, much understood –
He feels newly alive,
Under the spell of past time,
In this sad, lofty, pure
Epic tale of his life.

And the grey, country woman
As an old, kindly mother
Gives him her embrace.
He throws down his pen and he paces
Alone in his room;
And in his heart strives to grasp
What is understood only
By the very young and the old.

[1957]

In a letter to his son (6 June 1944) Zabolotsky recounts the episode, rendered with some additional detail in the poem. 'At first', he writes, 'I did not even understand what this was about [...] She explained that one son had been killed in the war, and that the second had been buried here two weeks before and now she was alone in the world [...] You se how much suffering there is. And yet people live and are even able to help others. There is much to be learnt from this old woman, who, observing the old Russian custom, offered me, a prisoner, a writer, her funeral alms. [...] The news has just arrived that the allies have landed in the South of France. We may hope that the end of the war is not far off.'

THE ABOMINABLE SNOWMAN

They say that, in the Himalayas,
Higher than temple or monastery,
There lives the primordial fosterling
Of beasts, a mystery to man.

White, serene, and shaggy-haired,
From time to time, from the heights
He descends, frolicking like a thing possessed,
And playing snowballs at the gates.

But when the Buddhist monks
Sound their trumpets from the walls,
He makes off, in fear and consternation,
To the safety of his mountain halls.

If these tall tales are not sheer nonsense,
It means that, even in our omniscient times,
This last half-beast, half-human
Has managed somehow to survive.

Clearly his intelligence is not vast,
And bleak is his refuge above the clouds,
Nor does this trapper of beasts possess
School, pagoda, or idol-house.

Safe in his mountain fastness,
It seems he does not even know
That loyal to their masters,
They're stockpiling atom bombs below.

Never will this Himalayan troglodyte
Discover their secret, even if
He plunge like an asteroid,
Blazing, into the abyss.

But while the lamas lament and chant
Over the fresh tracks in the snow,
And while the drums furiously
Beat in their temples below,

And while the thousand-years old Buddha
Tells fortunes and contemplates his navel,
In his remote sanctuary,
He feels comparatively cheerful.

Squatting by the spring, no doubt,
He is skinning a mountain deer,
While the only words he utters there
Are pronouns, as he laughs out loud.

[1957]

THUNDERSTORM

A scowling cloud interposes itself,
Covering half the distant sky.
Huge and unhurrying it moves,
A lantern lifted high.

How many times did it trap me,
How many times, gleaming with silver,
Did it hurl its broken bolts,
Unroll its stony thunder!

How often, anxiously crossing a field
Was I brought to a timorous halt,
Standing there, drawn against my will
Into that dazzling voltaic arc.

Close by our balcony, there it is:
A cedar, cleft by lightning.
And its lifeless canopy
Props up the dark horizon.

Through its living heart
A fiery wound courses.
Scorched needles rain down,
Like stars, or curses!

Sing to me, tree of sorrow!
Like you, I broke through into the heights,
But there was only lightning to greet me,
Scorching me in flight.

Split in two, like you, I did not die –
Why, I shall never understand –
In my heart the same fierce hunger,
And love, and singing till the end!

[1957]

IF, WEARY OF EXISTENCE

If, weary of existence,
I were just a silent corpse,
I'd no longer be subject
To human passions, simple, coarse.

Clay I might be, a mere handful,
Or transformed into a jug,
Which little country lasses
Carry with them to the spring.

Listening in on people's secrets
And the roll-call of the birds,
Among them, I'd be only
A chance combination of parts.

But even then, in the outer darkness,
Alone, communing with myself,
I'd laud this sinful existence,
Summoning it as I dreamt.

[1957]

IN MUCH WISDOM IS NO LITTLE GRIEF

In much wisdom is no little grief:
So said the author of Ecclesiastes.[1]
I am no sage, but why do I so often
Feel pity for the world and for mankind?

Nature wants to live and that is why
It feeds the birds seeds in their millions.
But towards the stars and summer-lightning
Scarcely a single bird has ever soared.

Foam-spattered, the seas cry out.
The universe is clamouring for beauty.
But in the graveyards, over tumuli,
Only the chosen flowers shine.

Am I only I? But a moment
Amid other existences. O, righteous God,
Why did you create the world, both cruel and good,
And give me a mind, that I might understand it!

[1957]

1. Ecclesiastes, 1: 18: 'For in much wisdom is much grief: and he that increaseth
   knowledge increaseth sorrow.' I have taken liberties with the King James Version.

AT DANTE'S TOMB[1]

Florence was a step-mother to me,
I wanted to lay my bones in Ravenna.
Passer-by, speak not of treachery,
Even upon that, let death set its seal.

Over my white burial-vault,
The dove coos, mellifluous bird.
Until now I have dreamt of my country,
Until now have been loyal only to it.

The broken lute does not accompany
The march, dead in its own camp.
Why, my unhappiness, my Tuscany, do you
Plant kisses upon my orphaned mouth?

But the dove explodes from the roof,
As though it feared some person,
And the evil shadow of a plane
Describes circles above the town.

So, bell-ringer, ring your bells!
The world's awash in blood, do not forget!
I wanted to lay my bones in Ravenna,
But even Ravenna would not have me.

[1958]

1. The Latin epithet on Dante's grave in Ravenna ends with the following verse: 'Here
   I lie, Dante, exiled from my own land, / He whom Florence, which gave birth to
   him, deprived of a mother's love.'

The Story of My Imprisonment

Nikolay Zabolotsky

translated by Robin Milner-Gulland

It happened in Leningrad on 19 March 1938. Miroshnichenko, Secretary of the Leningrad branch of the Union of Writers, summoned me to the office on urgent business. In his room sat two men I did not know, dressed in plain clothes.

'These comrades want a word with you,' said Miroshnichenko. One of the strangers showed me his NKVD card.

'We're going to have to have a talk with you at your home,' he said. In the car they had waiting for me we travelled to my home by the Griboyedov Canal. My wife was ill in bed in our room with angina. I told her what was happening. The NKVD man showed me a warrant for my arrest.

'So this is what we have come to!' I said, embracing my wife and showing her the warrant.

The search began. They sorted out two cases full of books and manuscripts. I said my farewells to my family. My small daughter was then eleven months old. As I kissed her she whispered 'Daddy!' for the first time. We went out and walked along the corridor to the staircase. Thereupon my wife rushed after us with a cry of horror. At the front door we parted.

I was taken to the Remand Prison [DPZ in Russian] attached to the so-called 'Big House' on Liteyny Prospekt. I was searched, my suitcase, scarf, braces and collar were taken away, the metal buttons were cut off my suit and I was locked into a tiny cell. After a short time I was ordered to leave my things in another cell and was taken along the corridors to interrogation.

There began an interrogation that lasted about four days and nights without a break. Hard upon the first words came abuse, shouting and threats. Since I refused to admit to having committed any sort of crime, they took me out of the normal investigators' room, and thereafter the interrogation was mostly conducted in the office of my personal investigator, Nikolay Nikolayevich Lupandin, and his deputy, Merkuryev. The latter had been brought in to assist the NKVD officials, who at the time could not cope with their work because of the large number of those arrested.

The investigators wanted me to admit to my crimes against Soviet authority. Since I knew of no such crimes that I had committed there was naturally nothing for me to confess.

'Do you know what Gorky said about enemies who won't surrender?' asked my investigator. 'They have to be destroyed!'

'That has no bearing on me,' I answered.

The reference to Gorky was repeated every time that some other investigator came into the office and learnt that I was a writer.

I protested against my unmerited arrest, against the rough treatment, the shouting and the abuse; I referred to the rights which I, like every citizen, enjoyed under the Soviet constitution.

'The Constitution stops operating at our front door,' answered the investigator mockingly.

During the first few days they beat me, trying to destroy me morally and exhaust me physically. I was not given food. I was not allowed to sleep. The investigators worked in shifts, while I sat motionless on a chair in front of their desk for days and nights on end. Through the wall, from the next office, someone's frantic shrieks could be heard from time to time. My legs began to swell, and on the third day I had to pull off my shoes, since I could no longer stand the pain in my feet. Consciousess started to dim, and I concentrated all my powers on answering rationally and not letting slip any wrong word relating to the people I was being questioned about. However, the interrogation sometimes stopped and we sat in silence. The investigator would write down something, I would attempt to sleep – but he would wake me up immediately.

In the course of the interrogation it emerged that the NKVD was trying to build up a case against some kind of counter-revolutionary writers' organization. N.S. Tikhonov[1] was supposed to be made the head of this organization. It was claimed that its

---

1. Nikolay Tikhonov (1896–1979), notable poet of the Russian Civil War, subsequently active in editorial work and in Soviet literary politics; President of the Writers Union 1944–46.

members included various Leningrad writers who had already been arrested: Benedikt Lifshits, Elena Tager, Georgy Kuklin, I think Boris Kornilov, somebody else and finally, myself. Great efforts were made to obtain information about Fedin and Marshak. Mention was often made of N.M. Oleynikov, T.I. Tabidze, D.I. Kharms and A.I. Vvedensky – poets with whom I had been linked by old ties of friendship and common literary interests. Particular fault was found with my long poem *Triumph of Agriculture* which had been published by Tikhonov in the journal *Zvezda* in 1933. 'Depositions' by Lifshits and Tager 'unmasking' me were read out but I was not allowed to read them with my own eyes. I demanded a face-to-face confrontation with Lifshits and Tager but did not get it.

On the fourth day, as a result of nervous tension, hunger and lack of sleep, I gradually began to lose my reason. As I recall, I myself was by now shouting at the investigators and threatening them. Signs of hallucination appeared: on the wall and the parquet floor of the office I saw some sort of figures in continual motion. I remember that once I was sitting before a whole conclave of investigators. I was no longer the least afraid of them and held them in contempt. Before my eyes the pages of some huge imaginary book were being turned, and I saw different illustrations on every page. Paying no attention to anything else, I was expounding the contents of these illustrations to my investigators. It is hard now to define the condition I was in, but I recollect experiencing a sense of inner relief and exaltation that these people had not succeeded in making a dishonourable man of me. Evidently consciousness was still flickering within me if I could memorize those circumstances and recall them to this day.

I do not know how long this went on. Finally they threw me out into another room. Stunned by a blow from behind, I fell down; I began to get up, but a second blow followed to the face. I lost consciousness. I came to, choking on the water that someone was pouring over me. Someone picked me up and, so it seemed, began pulling my clothes off. Again I lost consciousness. Hardly had I come round again than some characters whom I did not know started dragging me along the stone corridors of the prison, hitting me and mocking my defencelessness. They pulled me into a cell with an iron mesh door, whose floor was lower than that of the corridor, and locked me in. When I recovered (I do not know how soon that occurred) my first thought was: let me defend myself!

Defend myself, so as not to let these people kill me, or at least not give my life away for nothing! In the cell there stood a heavy iron bed. I dragged it to the mesh door and propped it under the doorhandle. So that the handle could not come away from the bedstead I tied them together with the towel that I had been wearing instead of a scarf. While busy with this I was surprised by my tormentors. They hurled themselves at the door so as to undo the towel but I grabbed a mop that was standing in the corner, and using it as a lance I defended myself as best I could; soon I had chased all the warders away from my door. To get the better of me they had to drag along a fireman's hose and get it into action; the high-pressure jet of water struck me and scorched my body. They used this jet to push me into a corner, and after lengthy efforts a whole crowd of them burst into the cell. Thereupon I was severely beaten up and kicked with jack-boots; subsequently the doctors were amazed that my internal organs were still intact, so severe were the marks of my ordeal.

I came to from a dreadful pain in my right arm. I lay with my arms tied to the iron bedstead behind my back. One of the cross-bars was biting into my arm and hurting me intolerably. I imagined that the room was being flooded with water, that its level was rising every moment and that it was about to cover me, head and all. I yelled in desperation and demanded that some governor of the prison should order me to be freed. This went on for an interminable time. Afterwards all became confused in my consciousness. I recollect that I came round on a wooden bunk-bed. Everything around was wet: my clothes were soaked through, and near by lay my jacket, also soaking wet and heavy as a stone. Thereafter I remember, as if in a dream, that people hauled me under the arms across a yard.... When consciousness again returned I was already in a hospital for the insane.

The prison hospital of the Institute of Forensic Psychiatry stood not far from the Remand Prison. Here, if I am not mistaken, I was held for about two weeks, first in a violent then in a quiet ward.

My condition was grave: I was shattered and no longer a responsible human being, while I was physically a wreck from my torments, from hunger and from lack of sleep. But a glimmer of consciousness still flickered within me or returned from time to time. Thus I well remember how appalled the nurse was as she took my clothes away: her hands and lips were trembling. I neither remember, nor indeed know, how I was treated in the initial stages.

I recollect only that I drank whole cupfuls of some thickish liquid that made my head seem wooden and insensible. In my first fit of despair I hastened to tell the doctors about all that had happened to me, but they merely kept saying: 'Calm down! Then you'll be able to justify yourself in court.' During those days the hospital was my refuge, and the doctors, even if they did not give me much in the way of treatment, at least did not torture me. Among them I remember Dr Gontarev and the woman doctor Nina Kelchevskaya.

Among the patients I recall one lunatic who, imitating a loudspeaker, often used to stand at the head of my bed glorifying Stalin in a trumpetlike voice. Another ran around on all fours, barking like a dog. These were the most disturbed of the patients. Madness descended upon the others only from time to time. Normally they kept quiet, smiling sarcastically or gesticulating, or lay motionless on their beds.

After a few days I began to get better and realized with horror that I should soon have to return to the place of torment. This occurred on one of the medical rounds, when in answer to the doctor's question as to how I came by the black contusions on my body I answered: 'I fell down and bruised myself.' I noticed the doctors glance round at each other: it was clear that consciousness had come back to me – I no longer wished to put the blame on the investigators, so as not to worsen my own position. However, I was still very weak, psychologically unstable, and found every breath I took difficult and painful, and these circumstances postponed my discharge for a few days.

On my return to the prison I was expecting to be taken to interrogation again, and made myself ready for anything so long as I did not incriminate either myself or others. I was not, however, taken to interrogation; instead I was thrown into one of the large common cells filled to bursting with prisoners. It was a big room intended for twelve to fifteen men, with a mesh door giving onto the prison corridor. There were seventy to eighty people in it, sometimes rising to a hundred. Clouds of steam and the special prison stench reached me in the corridor, and I remember being astonished by it. They could hardly shut the door after me, and I found myself in a crowd of people wedged tight against each other or sitting in disorderly heaps all over the room. Learning that the newcomer was a writer, my neighbours informed me that the cell contained other writers too, and soon they brought along P.N. Medvedev and D.I. Vygodsky, who had been arrested before me.

Seeing the sad state I was in, my comrades fixed me up a place in some corner. Thus began my prison life in the proper sense.

There are certain common characteristic signs that distinguish the majority of free people from the unfree. The former are sufficiently self-confident, have more or less a sense of their own worth, and react to external irritations calmly and sensibly. In the years of my imprisonment the average person, deprived of his liberty without due cause, humiliated, insulted, frightened and knocked out of his senses by the fantastic environment into which he had suddenly come, more often than not would lose the individuality that in freedom was his. Like a hare in a trap he would rush around helplessly, pushing at open doors, pleading his innocence, trembling with fear before worthless degenerates, losing his human qualities; he would be suspicious of everybody, would lose faith in those nearest him and would himself reveal his own lowest qualities, previously hidden from outsiders. After a few days of prison treatment the features of a slave would be clearly apparent on his countenance, and the lie foisted upon him would begin to put down roots in his confused and trembling soul.

In the Remand Prison, where people were held only during the period of investigation, this process of spiritual decay was only just beginning in people. Here one could observe all aspects of despair and all the manifestations of numbed hopelessness, of convulsive hysterical joy and of cynical indifference to everything in the world, including one's own life. It was strange to see these grown men now groaning, now fainting, now shaking with fear, persecuted and pitiable. I was told that the writer Adrian Pistrovsky, who had been in the cell not long before me, lost any human appearance in his grief, flung himself about the cell, scarred his chest with some sort of nail and at night got up to shameful things for all the cell to see. But in this respect the record was apparently held by Valentin Stenich, who was in the adjoining cell. An aesthete, snob and gourmand in ordinary life, by the accounts of the prisoners he quickly found a common language with the investigators, and for a packet of cigarettes would sign any sort of testimony. In fairness one must say that alongside such people there were others who maintained their human dignity at the expense of the greatest efforts. Often these decent people had until their arrest been humble cogs in our society, while the great of the world were frequently changed in prison into the pitiful semblance of men. Prison purified people but not in the sense that Zakovsky[2] and his fellow bosses wanted.

This process of human disintegration went on before the eyes of the whole cell. A man could not be alone here for a single moment, and he even had to attend to his needs at an open lavatory in the same place. He who wanted to weep wept in public, and the sense of natural shame made his pain ten times worse. He who wanted to commit suicide was obliged to grit his teeth and at night, under his blanket, attempt to open his veins with a splinter of glass – but somebody's sleepless eyes used quickly to discover the would-be suicide, and his comrades would disarm him. This life in public was an additional torment, but at the same time it assisted many to live through their intolerable sufferings.

The cell in which I found myself was like a huge, perpetually buzzing anthill, where all day long people trampled about in close proximity, breathed in each other's exhalations; they had to step over prostrate bodies as they walked, quarrelled and made peace, wept and laughed. Ordinary criminals were mixed in with the politicals; but in 1937–8 the politicals were ten times more numerous, and thus the criminals behaved timidly and unselfconfidently in the prison. In the camps they were our overlords, but in prison they were scarcely noticeable. In charge of our cell there was an elected leader called the Hetman. On him depended the ordering of our lives. He allocated places – where one was to sleep and sit – according to one's length of imprisonment, apportioned rations and supervised good order. Full agreement and discipline were needed to arrange everyone for the night. Space was such that people could lie down only on their side, jammed tight against each other, and even then not all at once but in two shifts. Night arrangements were carried out at the leader's command, and it was an astonishing performance of regulated, precisely calculated movements and transpositions worked out by many 'generations' of prisoners who had had to live in a tight-pressed throng and who gradually passed on their acquired skills to newcomers.

By day the cell lived a sluggish and tedious life Every trivial hum-drum action – sewing on a button, mending torn clothes,

2. L.M. Zakovsky, the notorious head of the Leningrad NKVD, himself subsequently executed.

going to the lavatory – grew into a major problem. Thus to go to the lavatory one had to wait in a queue for not less than half an hour. Interest was brought into the daily routine only by breakfast, lunch and supper. In the Remand Prison the food was tolerable, and the prisoners did not go hungry. Searches were another form of entertainment. They took place regularly and were of a humiliating nature. They only partially fulfilled their purpose, since every prisoner knew dozens of ways to hide his needle, his pencil-end or (greatest treasure of all) his penknife or razor-blade. Prisoners were scarcely ever summoned to interrogation during the day.

Interrogation used to begin at night, when the whole multi-storey façade on Liteyny Prospekt was flooded with hundreds of lights, and hundreds of sergeants, lieutenants and captains of the State Security together with their assistants got down to their routine tasks. The vast stone courtyard of the building, overlooked by the open windows of the offices, was filled with the groans and soul-rending screams of men being beaten up. The whole cell shuddered as if an electric current had suddenly passed through it, and dumb terror would again appear in the eyes of the prisoners. So as to drown these screams they often stationed heavy lorries in the courtyard with their engines running. But beyond the roar of the engines our imaginations pictured something already totally indescribable and our nervous agitation reached an extreme pitch.

From time to time one of the prisoners would be fetched out for interrogation. He would be summoned in the following way:

'Ivanov!' the warder would yell, coming up to the mesh door.

'Vasily Petrovich!' the prisoner would have to answer, giving the first two names.

'To the investigator!'

The prisoner would be taken out of the cell, searched and led along corridors to the NKVD building. In all the corridors there had been set up tightly-sealed wooden cabins, rather like cupboards or telephone-boxes. To avoid meeting other detainees who might appear at the end of the corridor the prisoner would normally be pushed into one such cabin, where he would have to wait till the other man had been led past.

From time to time those who had already been interrogated returned to the cell, sometimes they were pushed inside in complete prostration, while others almost had to be carried in, and subsequently we would spend a long time caring for these unfortunates, giving them cold compresses and water to drink. Moreover it often happened that a warder would come merely to collect a prisoner's belongings, while the prisoner called to interrogation did not return to the cell.

Mockery and blows were the lot of those who at that time conducted themselves otherwise than the way the interrogator wanted: that is, those who simply did not wish to denounce others.

D.I. Vygodsky, a most honourable man, a talented writer and already old, was dragged by the beard and spat upon in the face by an investigator. A sixty-year-old profesor of mathematics, my neighbour in the cell, with a disease of the liver, was made to get down on hands and knees by a sadistic investigator and kept in this position for hours on end, so as to exacerbate his illness and cause intolerable sufferings. Once on the way to interrogation I was accidentally pushed into the wrong office and saw a beautiful young woman in a black dress hitting an investigator in the face; he seized her by the hair, threw her to the floor and started to kick her with his boots. I was at once hauled out of the room, and behind my back I heard her terrifying screams.

How did the prisoners try to explain these perversions of the legal process, these inhuman tortures and torments? Most of them were convinced that they had genuinely been mistaken for major criminals. There were tales of one unfortunate who at every beating-up frantically yelled, 'Long live Stalin!' Two fellows would hit him with rubber truncheons wrapped in newspaper and he, writhing with pain, glorified Stalin, wishing that way to demonstrate his orthodoxy. The shadow of a guess flickered through the minds of the most sensible, and others were evidently not far from a true understanding of the matter, but all such people, persecuted and terrorized, dared not share their thoughts with each other, since not without reason they assumed that spies and secret informers, willing and unwilling, were busy in the cell. In my own head there grew the curious conviction that we were in the hands of the fascists, who right under the noses of our authorities had managed to liquidate the Soviet citizens at the centre of the penal system. I confided this guess of mine to an old Party member who was sitting beside me, and with terror in his eyes he admitted to me that he thought the same, but had never dared mention it to anyone. And indeed how else could we explain those horrors that were happening around us – we Soviet people, brought up in a spirit of dedication to the cause of socialism? Only now, eighteen years later, has life at last shown me how far we were right and how far we were wrong.

After my return from hospital I was left in peace and not called before the investigator for some time. When interrogations did begin again – and there were still a few to come – no one hit me any more, and things were limited to the ordinary threats and abuse. Finally in August I was summoned 'with my belongings' and transferred to the Kresty Prison.

I remember the boiling hot day when, dressed in a thick woollen coat and carrying a roll of underclothing, I was brought to a small cell at Kresty intended for two people. Ten bare human figures, running with sweat and exhausted from the heat, squatted like Indian gods all round the edge of the cell. I greeted them, stripped off and sat down as the eleventh in their midst. Soon there appeared beneath me a great damp patch on the stone floor. So began my life at Kresty.

In the cell stood one iron bed and on it slept a captain of the Northern Fleet, the recognized cell leader. His legs, injured during interrogation at Archangel, were no more use. The old sea-dog, who had habitually looked death in the eye, was now helpless as a baby.

At Kresty I was not interrogated: evidently the investigation was at an end. The food got suddenly and sharply worse, and if we had not had the right to buy extra foodstuffs with our own money we should have been half-starved.

At the beginning of October I was informed by note that I had been sentenced by a Special Commission (that is, without trial) to five years in a concentration camp for 'Trostkyite counter-revolutionary activity'. On 5 October I informed my wife of this and was permitted a meeting with her: a speedy departure on the journey was expected.

The meeting took place at the end of the month. My wife conducted herself sensibly, though she and the young children were already being banished from the city and my fate was unknown to her. She gave me a bag with essentials and we parted, not knowing if we should see each other again.

The convict train got under way on 8 November, the day after my family's departure from Leningrad. We were taken in heated waggons under heavy guard, and a couple of days later found ourselves at the Sverdlovsk transit prison, where we stayed about a month. On 5 December, the Day of the Soviet Constitution, we began our great Siberian journey – a whole odyssey of fantastic experiences that deserves to be recounted in greater detail.

They transported us with precautions appropriate not to ordinary, beaten, unfortunate folk but to some sort of superhuman villains, capable at any moment of blowing up the whole world, were we to take a single free step. Our train, an endless succession of prison wagons, presented an outlandish sight. On the roof were set up searchlights that lit up the whole area. At various places above and between the wagons machine-guns stuck out, there were guards in great numbers, and at halts they released alsatian dogs, ready to rend an escaper limb from limb. On those rare days when we were taken to the bath-house or transferred anywhere they ranged us in lines, made us kneel in the snow and put our hands behind our backs. In that position we would wait until the checking procedure was over, while all around dozens of rifle muzzles peered out at us and behind, pressing at our very heels, the dogs howled furiously and strained at the leash. We were made to march in close file.

'One step aside and I open fire!' was the usual warning.

Actually, in the entire two-month journey we got out only at Novosibirsk, Irkutsk and Chita. It goes without saying that no one else was allowed within a mile of us.

Sixty and more days we toiled along the main Siberian line, lingering in sidings for days at a time. There were some forty men in the wagon, as I recollect. A fierce winter had started and the frosts got deeper every day. A little iron stove was kindled in the centre of the wagon; the orderly sat near by and looked after it. At first we had lived on two levels – one half underneath, the other half above on high plank bunks ranged along the sides of the wagon, a little lower than a man's height. But soon the cold drove all those below on to the planks; even here, however, packed into a heap for bodily warmth, we suffered cruelly from the cold. Bit by bit life turned into purely physiological existence without higher interests, where a man's entire concerns were reduced to not dying of hunger or thirst, not freezing through and not being shot like a rabid dog.

Each man received 300 grammes of bread a day, hot water twice a day and a dinner of thin 'balanda' [soup] with a ladle of gruel. For starving and frozen men this food was of course not enough. But even this pitful ration was given out irregularly – and evidently not always through the fault of the privileged criminal prisoners who served it to us. The fact was that the provisioning of this whole vast mass of prisoners moving at that period through Siberia in endless echelons presented a complex economic problem. At many stations severe cold and poor administration made it impossible to supply men even with water. Once we received no water for about three days, and as we greeted the new year of 1939 somewhere around Lake Baykal we had to lick black sooty icicles that had formed on the walls of the wagon from our own exhalations. I shall never manage to forget this New Year's Day feast to the end of my life.

In that wagon I first came up against the world of criminals, who became the bane of life to us who had to drag out our lives beside them, and often under their command.

Criminals – recidivists, thieves, robbers, bandits, murderers, with their whole multifarious retinue of sympathizers, assistants and accomplices of various hues and shades – are a people apart, forming a long-established social category that has worked out its own way of life, its own moral code and even its own aesthetic. These men lived by their own laws, and these laws of theirs were stronger than those of any government. They had their own leaders, one word from whom could cost the life of any rank-and-file member of their caste. They were all linked by a common view of life, and for them view and practice of life were one. Original inhabitants of the prisons and camps, they deeply and genuinely despised us: a motley, variegated and disorientated crowd of chance visitors to their ultramontane world. From their point of view we were pitiful creatures, unworthy of respect and meriting the most merciless exploitation and death. And on occasions, when it was in their power, they would destroy us with a clear conscience and with the blessing, direct or indirect, of the camp authorities.

I hold to the opinion that a considerable proportion of the criminal fraternity are in fact exceptional people. These are men of outstanding capabilities that for one reason or another have been developed in a criminal direction, hostile to the rational norms of the human community. In the name of their moral code almost all of them are capable of remarkable, at times heroic feats; they would go to their deaths fearlessly, since the contempt of their comrades was for them a hundred times more terrible than any death. In my time, however, the mightiest leaders in the criminal world had already been eliminated. Legends about them were currrent and the entire criminal population of the camps saw in these legends their ideals and tried to live according to the precepts of their heroes. There were no more mighty leaders, but their ideology was alive and unscathed.

Somehow of its own accord, our wagon divided into two groups: those sentenced under Article 58 settled on one side,[3] the criminals on the other. Condemned to co-exist, we stared at each other with concealed hostility, and only occasionally did this hostility break through to the surface. I remember how once, without any provocation from my side, one of our criminals who was liable to fits and some sort of instantaneous hysteria attacked me with a log of wood. His comrades restrained him and I was unharmed. But an atmosphere of peculiar psychological tension never left us for a moment, and put its stamp upon our life in the train.

From time to time the authorities appeared in the wagon to carry out a check to verify the numbers. At a special command we had to crawl across a board to the other ledge, and they counted us as we did so. The picture is as vivid before me as if it were happening now: black with soot, beards sprouting, we crawl one after the other on all fours like monkeys across the board, lit by the dim glow of lanterns, while a semi-literate guard holds us at rifle point and counts and counts away, getting muddled in his tricky calculations.

Insects devoured us, and the two baths arranged for us at Irkutsk and Chita did not deliver us from this affliction. Both these baths were sheer torment. Each was like an inferno filled with a wildly cackling throng of devils large and small. There was not the remotest possibility of washing. One felt lucky if one managed to save one's personal posessions from the professional criminals. Loss of possessions indicated almost certain death on the journey. This indeed happened to certain unfortunates: they died without reaching camp. In our wagon there were no fatal incidents.

For more than two months our mournful train dragged its way along the main Trans-Siberian line. Two small iced-up windows under the ceiling allowed faint light into our wagon during the short hours of daylight. At other times a candle-end glowed in a lantern, and when candles were not given out the whole wagon was plunged into impenetrable darkness. Pressed tightly together we lay in this primordial gloom, listening to the thudding of the wheels and sunk in disconsolate thoughts about our fate. In the mornings we could only just manage to peer out of the window at the limitless expanse

3. Article of the Criminal Code of the RSFSR (On Counter-Revolutionary Crimes) under which political prisoners were normally sentenced; repealed in 1958.

of the Siberian fields, the endless snow-covered forests, the shadowy villages and towns, watched over by columns of vertical smoke, the fantastic sheer cliffs of the shores of Lake Baykal. We were being taken further and further towards the Far East, towards the end of the world.

In the first days of February we arrived at Khabarovsk. Here we stopped a long time. Then we were suddenly moved backwards, reached Volochaevka and turned northwards off the main line along a newly built branch. Along both sides of the railway there were glimpses of camps with their watch-towers and settlements of modern 'gingerbread houses' all built to the same pattern. The kingdom of the BAM[4] was meeting us, its new settlers. The train stopped, there was a rattling of bolts, and we stepped out from our hiding-places into this new world, flooded in sunlight, shackled in a frost of minus fifty, encircled with the apparitions of slim Far Eastern birch-trees rising to the very heavens.

Thus we came to the town of Komsomolsk-on-the-Amur.

This translation was first published in *The Times Literary Supplement*, 9 October 1981.

4. The Baykal–Amur Railway, then under construction.

My Father

Nikita Zabolotsky

translated by Daniel Weissbort

My father Nikolay Aleseyevich Zabolotsky belonged to the first post-Revolution generation of Russian writers. It is important to remember this, as from the 1920s the Bolshevik government actively and cruelly interfered in the creative life of the intellegentsia, subjecting it to the official ideology and insisting on its support in achieving the Party's political objectives. Those writers whose personality was formed before this historical watershed were freer from the start – both in themselves and in realizing their creative potential, although this made life no easier for them during the Soviet era. Such celebrated figures as Pasternak, Mandelstam, Akhmatova, Tsvetayeva were eleven to fourteen years older than Zabolotsky, and had received their education and published their first collections of poetry before the Revolution. In 1917, Zabolotsky was only fourteen years old, a student in the secondary school in the small town of Urzhum in Vyatka Province, located at a considerable distance from the main cultural centres of the Russia of that time.

Nethertheless, his pre-revolutionary childhood undoubtedly influenced the poet's later artistic development. At the end of the 1940s, he remarked: 'Our character is formed before the age of five to six. I am sure of that, and afterwards, a protective covering is adopted. There has to be something to protect, and then adaptability and an amazingly stubborn instinct for self-preservation combine. [...] However this adaptability has to be strictly contained, or everything goes to hell!' Zabolotsky was raised in the family of an agronomist, on the *zemstvo* farms where his father worked – before 1909 this was near Kazan, then in Sernur (now in the Mari Autonomous Republic) and Urzhum. An ongoing relationship with nature, his father's work, familiarity with the life of the peasantry, the pagan beliefs of the Mari, chemical experiments in the little laboratory, books in his father's library, involvement in theatrical and literary circles – this is what formed the young poet's personality. In his autobigraphical essay he wrote: 'As a seven year-old child, I had already chosen my future profession.' He later wrote, addressing his muse fatalistically:

> It was you who chose me,
> Who got into my soul,
> Opened my eyes
> To the wonders of the earth...
> ('The Blind Man', 1946)

My father remained true to his vocation, and no obstacle was allowed to turn him from the path chosen in childhoood. He valued this constancy in himself and would often try to instil it in us children: 'Money and fame come on their own, sooner or later,' he said. 'This is not what's important. What's important in life is to chose your work and carry it out with love, perseverance and craftsmanship... Drop by drop, drop by drop, but continuously and always on the same spot – and even the hardest rock is worn away!'

The basic theme of his work, the interrelationship and interaction of man and the nature surrounding him, he also no doubt took from his childhoood. He saw how the agronomist tried equally to improve agricultural methods and to overcome the conservatism of the peasantry. In the boy's mind, the agricultural worker merged with the surrounding nature and became, as it were, an integral part of it. Echoes of these impressions from childhood can be found in such works as 'Agriculture Triumphant', 'The Birds', 'Resting Peasants', 'The Deep Book', and many other poems.

After finishing secondary school in Urzhum, Nikolay left for Moscow, in 1920, and the following year Petrograd (Petersburg), to study and to join in contemporary literary life. As a student in the department of language and literature at the Pedagogical Intitute, he went hungry, working as a docker in the port, freezing in poorly heated lecture-theatres and lodgings, suffering from scurvy. It was hard for the young man to reconcile the noble aims of the Revolution with the ensuing famine, the tragedy of the recently ended civil war with the policy of 'turning the screws on' during the period of 'war communism'. At the end of 1921, in a state of moral confusion, he wrote to an Urzhum friend:

> It is senseless to weep and complain, ... but the gloomy lines almost write themselves:
>
>> In the funereal whistle of the revolution
>> Do you see the bloody fingers?
>> Thoughts groan, songs beat –
>> Do you hear?
>> ....
>> And we stand – disgraced shadows,
>> Obligatory coffin-makers of the times.
>
> A cursed, yes, cursed life! I have become entangled in its grey web, ensnared, and where is the way out?'

The New Economic Policy (NEP) introduced by the government did not much change the young man's life, but it did provide him with interesting material. The growing number of privately owned shops and restaurants, markets and second-hand goods stalls were filled with small traders and second-hand dealers hungry for profit. The luxury life of the *nouveau riche* entrepreneurs, the soulless bourgeois existence – all this was alien and repulsive to Zabolotsky. But as an artist he could not help feasting his eyes on the 'coarse and meaningless, but extremely tangible materialism, the Flemish carnality of this world' (D. Maksimov). An extreme reaction to this urban life, so detached from nature, helped him to develop an unusual, grotesque poetic style. Of course, this style was based also on previous literary experiments. Zabolotsky had studied some Russian and Western European literature and, as he wrote in his autobiographical essay, 'at one time I [even] thought of dedicating myself wholly to scholarship. But my attachment to poetry proved stronger and dreams of a scholarly life were abandoned.' Of the many poets studied by him one might pick out the eighteenth-century Russian ones, as well as Goethe, Baratynsky, Mandelstam and of course Khlebnikov.

'I finished the Institute in 1925', wrote Zabolotsky. 'To my name was a bulky notebook of bad poems; my possessions could easily fit into a small basket.' In future, self-discipline, persistent efforts at self-improvement, tireless intellectual striving and native talent filled in the gaps of his provincial education as well as that of his education at the Institute.

Two circumstances helped Zabolotsky to establish his own creative position and develop a distinct poetic form: his participation, between 1926 and 1928, in the literary group which at the end of 1927 was called 'Oberiu' (*Obedinenie realnovo iskusstva/* Association of Real Art), and his enthusiasm for the avant-garde painters Pavel Filonov, Kazimir Malevich, Marc Chagall. Later the circle of artists interesting him expanded to include Henri Rousseau, Breughel, Rokotov, Botticelli, Pirosmani etc. This interest in the graphic arts was no idle one: the poet learned to see the world through painter's eyes and to to think in terms of spatial images.

His closeness to fellow *Oberiuti* (Daniil Kharms, Aleksandr Vvedensky, Konstantin Vaginov et al.) and to leftist artists, helped Zabolotsky to enter into the stream of avant-garde art, which in 1926–30 defined his creative activity and in the following years enriched his poetry. However, he always dissociated himself from the aesthetic principles of the radical left and as the years went by increasingly valued the semantic content of poetry.

I remember once how my father, with pride in his youthful literary endeavours, told me about his association with the *Oberiu*: 'We set out on along a broad front, believing in our eventual success. Not only did we have our poetry, but we also had our theatre, music and even film...' Father did not talk about his reasons, towards the end of 1928, for leaving the *Oberiuty* and how the group was abused in the official press and disintegrated, several of its members being arrested in late 1931. In general he spoke little and only reluctantly of his youth and literary origins.

In 1929 his first small collection *Stolbtsy* (Columns) appeared (twenty-two poems, with a print run of 1200). About this collection, the literary critic B.A. Filippov, who emigrated to the USA, wrote: 'Men of letters, the student population of the capital, and the higher ranks of the intelligentsia took this work as a kind of revelation. After a month you could not find the book at any price. Fair copies were made, and it was literally learnt by heart. The present writer owns not only printed, but handwritten and typed copies of *Stolbtsy*.'

This year also saw the start of the forced collectivization of the countryside and of urban industrialization. To eliminate the alleged opposition of the so-called 'class enemy', repressive measures were intensified. It was not surprising that in these circumstances the few positive mentions of *Stolbtsy* were drowned out by a chorus of malicious, vulgarizing critics, hostile to any authentically new development and manifestation of independence in art. Critical articles were filled with political accusations and crude insults.

Despite this situation, between 1929 and 1933 there took place a particularly promising development in Zabolotsky's nature-philosophy, as it affected his creative work. All that existed, including man, seemed to him equally part of a single vast organism. In its present form, this organism had not yet achieved perfection – it was engaged in a permanent struggle for survival and at the same time its suffering spirit strove towards liberation from the dominion of 'the eternal winepress'. This tragic contradiction was to be resolved through the advance of the whole universe from chaos towards regulation, from egotism towards collective wisdom, from feral destructiveness to the celebration of Truth, Beauty and the Good. And this development was served by a consciousness inherent in nature, the highest expression of which was man's reason. Nature had created man for him to reveal the laws of perfectability, and with their help, to ensure a joyful, intelligent existence for all of creation. Reading the biblical legend of the apple, the fruit of the tree of knowledge, the poet thought about these wonderful laws. And he turned to the fruits of the earth:

> I should like to add you to my library,
> to read you and to disengage the law,
> Preserved by you...
> ['A Garlanding with Fruit', 1932]

Similar notions lay behind the long poems: 'Agriculture Triumphant', 'The Mad Wolf', 'The Trees', 'The Birds', 'The Clouds' (this has not survived) and various other poems, not only from the end of the 1920s and beginning of the 1930s, but from the later period as well. In developing his ideas, Zabolotsky read works by scholars and thinkers and was always gratified to find confirmation in them.

'Agriculture Triumphant' (1929–30) was published in the Leningrad magazine *Zvezda* (The Star) in 1929, in separate sections, and in 1933 in its entirety, but with amendments introduced by the censorship. These publications produced a new spate of attacks on Zabolotsky. He was accused of being an inveterate formalist, an enemy of rural socialist reforms, an apologist for counter-revolutionary ideology. His new book of poems, including part of *Stolbtsy* and the poem 'Agriculture Triumphant', was banned and the type, which had already been set, was broken down. Ominous political charges and the ban on publication finally persuaded him that his own original work would not be permitted to take its place in contemporary poetic life. From the second half of 1933 and through 1935 the poet suffered profound disillusionment, depression and a creative slump. At this time he concentrated on his work in children's literature and began to translate foreign poetry.

In summer 1936, the entire Zabolotsky family – Nikolay Alekseyevich, Ekaterina Vasilevna and their four-year-old son (a daughter, Natasha, was born the following year) – lived in the Ukraine. I remember the small, white family home, in the midst of an orchard with beehives between the trees, a veranda with hop-plants growing over it, and the landlady's black dog. A path led to the Dnieper River, skirting a solitary old oak-tree, in which huge hornets and horned stag-beetles lived. My father and I studied these remarkable insects, and he showed me how dung-beetles rolled perfect little balls in the dusty road, and how snails slithered along the sand-bars, with their calcified homes on their backs. Larks sang in the blue sky, grasshoppers chirred in the grass, yellowed from the heat. These scenes of nature with their calming effect, conducive to poetic reflection, in no way tallied with man's cruelty on this same earth.

It was here, in the Ukraine, that Zabolotsky first realized how barbaric were the methods being used to implement collectivization and how terrible was the famine among the Ukrainian peasantry in 1932–3. In poems written at the time, the theme of grief, anxiety, confusion were a natural consequence of the mental condition in which the poet had found himself in the last few years. In his 1936 poem 'Drought', for instance, he wrote:

> But my life is a hundred times more sad,
> when lonely reason ails,
> and monstrous fantasies squat there,
> lifting their snouts above the sedge.
> And the poor soul swoons,
> and, like snails, doubts crawl out...

Observing the life-giving activity of a squall and of a summer downpour, falling on plants laid low by drought, the poet looks to refresh his own spirit and exclaims: 'Do not be afraid of storms! Let nature's / cleansing force strike you midships!' But fate had an entirely different, and in no way cleansing storm in store for him...

It seemed, at the time, that Zabolotsky's life was finally working out – both materially and from a literary point of view. He had been in Georgia, completing a translation for children from the great twelfth-century Georgian poet Rustaveli, translating contemporary Georgian, Ukrainian and other poets, and writing his own poems. Several of the latter were favourably received by the official critics. This permitted him, in 1937, to publish his *Second Book*, seventeen poems in which the radical traits of his *Oberiu* period were no longer so discernible. Zabolotsky was a recogized poet now. Old and new literary friends supported him – N. Stepanov, N. Oleinikov, B. Eikhenbaum, Yu. Tynyanov, N. Tikhonov, V. Kaverin, E. Shvarts, A. Gitovich, S. Chikovani and others. On his desk lay the beginning of his translation of the Old Russian epic *Slovo o polky Igoreve* ('The Lay of Igor's Campaign'), his own historical poem *Osada Kozelska* ('The Siege of Kozelsk'; this projected epic about the Mongol assault on Kozelsk in 1239 has been lost), and new poems...

But at this point disaster disrupted the poet's normal life and work. On 19 March 1938, he was arrested by organs of the NKVD. At that time, the Stalin terror was spreading with unprecedented virulence, and the poet who had frequently been called an 'enemy', a 'wrecker', 'a kulak poet', in the press and at the first Congress of Writers, found himself in an exposed position. After the arrest, followed by four days of continuous interrogation without food or sleep, beatings, two weeks of psychiatric hospital and new interrogations, Zabolotsky mobilized all his moral and physical strength so as not to slander either himself or those against whom the investigators were trying to trump up cases. His conception of human dignity and poetic honour did not permit him to cross this line and so lose his self-respect. In the history of the investigations during the Soviet period this was comparatively rare, since Stalin's henchmen knew their job and how much a human being could endure. Zabolotsky followed the precept in Rustaveli's poem: 'Better an honorourable death, than shameful salvation!' and would not provide the investigators with the required 'testimony'.

Finally, absurdly, he was accused of having been involved in a 'right wing, anti-Soviet writers' organization since 1931' and having been 'the author of anti-Soviet works, which were made use of by a right-wing Trostkyite organization'. Although he did not admit any guilt, he was sentenced to five years correctional hard labour by a so-called Special Commission (*Osoboe soveshchanie*), that is without trial. He remained in the GULAG camps of the Far East, in the Altai Region, until August 1944, labouring in the stone quarries, felling trees in the *taiga*, and extracting sea salt. For a considerable part of the time, however, he worked as a draftsman in the building section of the camp. Learning the profession of draftsmen while in confinement certainly saved his life, since only the most healthy and robust individuals were able to withstand the years of continual physical work in camp conditions.

From spring 1945 until the end of the year, Zabolotsky was already living with his family in Karaganda (Kazakhstan), working in the camp's construction office and in his free time completing his translation of 'The Lay of Igor's Campaign', which he had begun before his arrest.

In 1946, thanks to friends' efforts on his behalf, he was reinstated in the Writers' Union and received permission to live in the capital. At the same time, organs of the state security secretly had him shadowed by informants ('secret service observation'), which he suspected, trying to be circumspect in conversation, so as not to bring new misfortunes to his family. The last, Moscow period of his work began.

For the first two years, with no home of their own, the family lived in Peredelkino, the resort village for writers near Moscow. Zabolotsky did not yet have any regular literary income, and it was not easy for the family to get by. To feed us, he dug up part of the field in front of the house and, with the permission of the dacha's owners, grew potatoes and other vegetables. 'For now I can rely only on my own potatoes,' he remarked ironically to the well-known writers who greeted him through the fence.

After his release from the camp he tried to convince himself, his wife and his friends that he would no longer write the poems that had brought him so much hardship, but would occupy himself solely with the translation of foreign poetry. But he was unable to keep this promise; as soon as a relatively tranquil life was re-established, he began to write poetry again. Some of the best poems of his Moscow period were written in Peredelkino: 'In This Birch

Grove', 'The Blind Man', 'Storm', 'Testament' etc. Zabolotsky's new poems, harmonious and classically lucid, to a large extent continued along the thematic lines that had been interrupted by his arrest. But now the connection between man and nature was expressed in plainer spiritual and moral terms, the spirituality of the surrounding world ('the spirit of nature') combined with that of the living human spirit. In one of his letters from the camp, Zabolotsky had written: 'The living human spirit alone has remained precious.' There was a nakedness, an autobiographical element in these poems, not characteristic of his work hitherto. The fates of people, expressions on the faces of human beings, inner psychological tension in landscapes, echoes of history in contemporary reality all interested the poet.

Unfortunately, the situation in the country and accordingly in literary life, at the end of the 1940s and beginning of the 1950s, did not encourage the realization of those creative possibilities Zabolotsky had been able to preserve and even develop during the years of confinement. On the contrary, with people being shadowed and innocents who had already served their camp terms being re-arrested, it was necessary to exercise caution and at times to refrain from writing down poems that had formed in his consciousness. There was a slump in his creative production between 1946 and 1948 and for three to four years he turned almost wholly to translation, mostly of Georgian poetry.

Zabolotsky was not arrested again, but in 1951 he received notice from the militia to leave Moscow within ten days, which in effect meant his literary excommunication. Only the protection of the Writers' Union leadership saved him from this new exile.

In the stifling social atmosphere of the time, my father tried hard to submerge the memories of what he had experienced and his uncertainties about the future in the pleasures of life and work that were accessible to him. He loved to invite friends and acquaintances to his cramped Moscow apartment, and to entertain them with food that Mother prepared, as well as with good Georgian wine, to talk, to read his few new poems or any translations that had been particularly successful. Sometimes for the amusement of all, he read his comic poems and laughed along with his guests.

He was a man of great dignity, sure of himself and of his poetic talent, unusually courteous, sometime ironical, and with a gentle sense of humour. He inspired respect in all those who came into contact with him, even more so if they knew him well. Behind the

appearance of calm, the punctiliousness, even formality, one
discerned penetrating powers of observation and that 'playfulness
of mind and spirit' that he tried to carry over into his poems, also
outwardly tranquil and dignified. And only his wife and closest
friends knew how hard it was for him to acknowledge that in other
circumstances he might have produced more and perhaps written
differently. However, he tried to rise above such thoughts and
believed that destiny knew what it was doing.

Only in 1956, when the so-called 'Khrushchev thaw' got under
way, did the situation in the country change significantly.
Zabolotsky began to feel less fettered, freer in his work, more able
to speak his mind. Significantly, between 1956 and 1958, he wrote
about half of all the poems of his Moscow period, some of them
being published in magazines and literary miscellanies. In 1957 his
last collection appeared, the most complete to be published during
his lifetime (64 poems and translations). But total freedom of
expression in Russia still lay a long way ahead.

In autumn 1957, as a member of a delegation of poets, he
travelled abroad for the first time – to Italy. Knowing that there
was a particular interest in Europe in the early poetry of Zabolotsky,
the president of the Writers' Union proposed that he bring with
him the little volume *Stolbtsy*. The head of the literature
department even said that it would be good to edit these poems and
that they could then be published in the context of the poet's
collected works. Zabolotsky took this to be an indication of his
political rehabilitation; after all, he had been permitted to travel
beyond the iron curtain for a first meeting with Italian poets and
the re-publication of *Stolbtsy* had been promised!

He had made some minor emendations to *Stolbtsy* and to several
earlier poems of the 1930s, but now it was a question of making
more basic changes in the text, smoothing out the especially abrupt
'clashes of meanings' and making the poems more intelligible to
the unsophisticated reader. He corrected the text, making
adjustments not only in the hope of publication, but also because
his own literary tastes had changed in thirty years. Zabolotsky
valued his early work, often making use of stylistic features of
Stolbtsy in his later poems, and in the last years of his life read his
poems of the 1920s and 1930s to friends with pleasure and a covert
pride. One should bear in mind also that not more than one poem
in three was revised in this fashion.

After the trip to Italy Zabolotsky intended to embark on major new projects that would expand the temporal context of his world vision. On the evening before he died, Father outlined to Mother what he would have liked to write during his lifetime. She passed this on to us:

> He said that he needed two years to assemble a trilogy of long poems: 'The Death of Socrates', 'The Adoration of the Magi', 'Stalin'. The subject of the third poem surprised me. Nikolay Alekseyevich started to explain that Stalin was a complex figure, at the point of intersection between two eras...

It has to be assumed that in the poems planned by my father, a distinctive view of the most tragic, critical moments in the development of our civilization would have found expression. In the last years of his life he wanted to show that without soul, without a highly developed moral sense and secure aesthetic foundations, reason would never be able to realize its high destiny, to create a harmonious world for the prosperity and well-being of of all creatures, including man. This is why he exhorted us (in his last poem) not to 'allow the soul to idle!'

On the morning of 14 October 1958, Nikolai Alekseyevich Zabolotsky died of a series of heart attacks. That day I noticed on his work-table a fresh sheet with these words clearly written on it:

1. Shepherds, animals, angels
2.

The second item remained blank.

To sum up, one must again stress that Zabolotsky lived in very problematical times. Essentially his whole life was a hidden, solitary struggle with the totalitarian regime. And it is not so easy to determine how much was unavoidably lost in this struggle. In any case, neither the brutal criticism of the 1930s, prison and camp, nor subsequent police shadowing during the Moscow period of his life, nor the oppressiveness of the official ideology, forced Zabolotsky to deviate from his independent line of thought and to abandon his commitment to his work. The small collection of his poems now has its assured place in the treasury of twentieth-century Russian poetry.